Faculty-led

360

Guide to Successful Study Abroad

Melanie McCallon & Bill Holmes

Faculty-led 360: Guide to Successful Study Abroad

Published by:
Agapy LLC
Charleston, Illinois
Website: http://www.agapy.com

Printed in the United States of America

International Standard Book Number: 978-0-9721328-7-9

Library of Congress Control Number: 2010938470

Table of Contents

Updates to this book:
Facultyled.com

Acknowledgements

From Melanie:

Too often we fail to recognize those who have mentored and inspired us to be where we are and become who we are. I have been fortunate to be surrounded by encouragement and support that kept reminding me anything is possible.

A bottomless thank you (and some coffee and cake) to Jennifer Dickey, Jolene Miesner, Katie Davidson, and Nichole Hunley, without whom none of this would have worked. Jim Carter, thank you for always dreaming big and believing we could do it. And to the countless faculty who have trusted me to help them along the way, thank you.

My co-author, Bill, you have a slew of crazy ideas that I can never say no to. Thank you for challenging me to create, to provide, and to help. Your support and encouragement as we have built, assessed, and revised programs, texts, and life, has been...fun.

Fred Miller, you were the first professor who took a real interest in my learning and advancement. You made me feel like I could do anything. When I came to MSU as a professional, you were my first cheerleader. Your mentoring has meant more than you will ever know. Your level-headedness has frequently calmed me and helped me see things clearly. Thank you for your honesty and openness, even when it was painful to hear.

Celia Wall, you and I came to a realization somewhere along the way that we could trust each other deeply and our work relation-ship fell into place quite easily after that. Thank you for bringing me into CCSA and for honoring me with your confidence even before I earned it. Your knowledge, support, and many ideas resulted in successes that I received credit for and not only did you not mind, but you wanted it that way. You have taught me humility and kindness in a way no one else ever could have. Thank you for your constant belief.

Mike Klembara, thank you. You have treated me like your own, just as you asked us at CCSA to do for our students. In so doing you taught me how to care for students before I knew what it was like to be a parent. You taught me how to be diligent in my research and transparent in my process. Thank you for allowing me to be a part of CCSA and for teaching me every day.

Bonnie Higginson, your collaboration on the Belize program was one of the most exciting things I had taken on in my days at MSU and taught me that we could do so much more. Thank you for not only opening those doors for me, but showing me that the doors even existed. Your spirit, contribution, support, and love for international education has given me the example I needed to see clearly that there are others out there who want to do this thing called study abroad.

Mike Basile, you trusted me. Even when you knew I was green, you took a chance on hiring me and letting me take the reins to see what I could do. You never said no. You always fought for me, and sometimes with me, to get me to slow down (I don't know that it ever worked). You always saw possibility in everything I explored and encouraged me to keep moving. I always knew you had my back in every decision. You have been my greatest mentor not only in the office but outside of it, too, as you encouraged me to keep a balance between work and home. I could never thank you enough.

My friends know that this text was one of many items on my to-do list. You helped me figure out how to juggle it all and cheered me through it. Thank you. I couldn't stand without you.

Luckily for me my retired English-teacher mom has been my cheerleader, editor, and mainstay. Dad just nods and laughs, and sometimes that's just what I need. Thank you, mom and dad. Kyle, you're the brother everyone dreams of having. I couldn't ask for more. Thank you. Dale, I am so thankful that Dylan has a dad who believes fatherhood is his greatest role. Thank you for your support as we worked through this massive task together.

And, Dylan, your references to 'your book' have become fond memories for me through this process. It has been the most normal thing in the world for you even when our schedule was anything but. Thank you for being you. You are exactly what I need.

From Bill:
None of this would have been possible without my best friend, my wife Erin. It is so nice to be married to someone much smarter than myself and who does not mind proofreading scores of pages for me. Thanks for not letting me watch TV when I wanted to and instead forcing me to focus on getting this done. I am also extremely blessed that I not only get to work with you every day on campus but that we get to spend our summers together abroad. We have it good.

Thanks to my parents, Clint and Marilyn, for supporting me through years of school and not charging me rent or for meals. Without them, I would probably still be working somewhere with a shovel in my hand rather than traveling around the world. However, sometimes I do long for my shovel-wielding days.

Thanks to my counterparts at the various universities across the ACA. Working with you, showed us the great need for a useful yet simple book for folks new to program development. I really appreciate the ACA's work to help make education abroad accessible to faculty and students in our unique region of America.

Major thanks to my office staff, John Honeycutt, Annette Males and Laura Cromer. If they were not so pleasant, intelligent, efficient, and motivated to cross jobs and help each other, we could never have accomplished all we have thus far. Thanks to them for proof-reading and giving feedback on various items.

I would like to give a shout out to the Peace Corps, for whom my wife and I spent two years as volunteers in Ukraine. It is thanks to that experience that I learned various proven steps that can be taken to promote an individual's health and safety abroad and intensify their cultural competence and language facility. If only everyone in the field of International Education could have this experience.

Special thanks to my partner in this project, Melanie McCallon, who worked with me to create my first program in Ukraine and who has since assisted me by delivering workshops at the ACA Summit over the past couple of years. If only everyone were as professional and committed to students as you are.

Thanks to Dr. Robert Doty for proofreading chapters on a moment's notice. Even greater thanks for the good coffee and discussions of world literature. It has kept me sane.

Thanks to the School for Field Studies. Attending the *Risk Management for Faculty Leading Short Term Programs & Working with Students/Managing Behavior* workshops a few years back was a formative experience. They provide an excellent service and I highly recommend their workshops.

From Both Melanie and Bill:
Thanks to the faculty, friends, and family who proofread our drafts and provided valuable input as we formulated this text.

And finally, a special thanks to the many people leading programs abroad who have provided lessons in what *not* to do.

Chapter One: Why Should I Do This?

Why do we take students abroad? Why should we take students abroad? Really, why should we? Why should universities support study abroad staff, insert international education into mission statements and strategic goals, and promote the idea of global citizenship? Why should faculty consider getting on a plane with 10 (or 50) students to teach a course abroad? What can students learn abroad that they can't learn at home? It's not hard to find a faculty leader who has been dealt a challenging program abroad; one fraught with lost luggage, delayed flights, and ill students. So, then, why keep going? Many of us have pondered these questions and come back with the same answer: the reward is far greater than the sacrifice.

Assuming you have picked up this book, you probably don't need to be convinced of why you should lead a study abroad program, but instead need some guidance on how. Spending time, then, convincing you to lead a study abroad program is beside the point. You have likely gone through the preliminary questions of why study abroad is important, why *you* should take students abroad, how to manage it around your personal and family life, and how to take on the added professional responsibilities of leading a faculty-led program with or without support from your institution. However, it may not have occurred to you how leading study abroad programs can advance your career, profession, department, university, and students—hence, the reason for this chapter.

1.1 Study Abroad Challenges you as a Teacher
Teaching on a study abroad program develops your ability to be innovative and creative. Striking a balance between the academics of the structured classroom and the academics of experiential learning can be challenging, but worthwhile. On the home campus, you have your classroom. When you are abroad, you have the entire city, culture, and more. Whether or not you have actual

meeting space, you are forced to think outside the box when formulating the next 'lecture.' The city *becomes* the classroom and you recognize teachable moments throughout the program. The experiential component of learning allows your students to have their hands on the culture and learn from a fresh perspective. Sitting in a US classroom looking at slides of Monet's work is hardly the same as strolling through the Musee D'Orsay to see the real thing.

For the professor who is accustomed to classroom lecture, however, the study abroad format can be difficult to manage. How do you teach your students everything they need to know when so much time is spent on activities and excursions? Do you need to lecture for three hours each day beforehand? Well, do you? Think about it. How can you reconfigure your course, your syllabus, and even your teaching style to match what can be learned on-site without an accompanying lecture? What alternative learning can take place to augment your syllabus and traditional text?

Faculty-led study abroad is about challenging yourself to explore new teaching methods and learning styles. Not to worry, students participating in your program will find plenty of ways to discover and learn, and you will find yourself growing, too. You are with your students daily; you have greater flexibility to teach throughout the experience, and the group will read what you have assigned before they even get on the plane. In short, your students will step up to the plate to learn the material and will get more than a textbook out of your class.

> There is nothing like being there...light bulbs turning on in students' heads, and fireworks going off, when their academics and experience converge.

Continual inner-processing is vital to the study abroad experience. When teaching abroad, it becomes your responsibility to coach students through the 'weird' and into the 'a-ha.' You are challenged as the faculty leader to help students reflect on and compare the many differences they experience, but not necessarily to be a know-it-all. Admit what you do not know and commit to discovering together with your students. They will enjoy seeing your a-ha moments as much as you will enjoy seeing theirs.

1.2 Personal and Professional Advancement

As educators, we have found that each time we lead students abroad, we discover something new. Leading students abroad is a phenomenal way to invest in ourselves as professionals and as cultured human beings. We have the opportunity to see our field from a new perspective and examine the way our students view the field as well. This spills over into how we teach at home.

The process of self-discovery is not only for students, it is for us, too. Leading students abroad allows us to learn things we did not know before and provides us with an opportunity for personal and professional development. It's not only about the students removing their blinders, but a time for us to see as well. When we travel alone, we have only the benefit of our own eyes, experience, and interpretation. However, when we travel in a group, we have the benefit of each participant's experience and interpretation combined with our own. This dynamic interaction can fuel extraordinary learning, growth, and development.

I spent four days in Belize with a group of seniors who were doing their student teaching abroad. It was the most insightful and open group of students I have ever experienced. Returning home on my 4-year-old son's birthday, my plane was delayed, and I had several hours to think about and journal my experience. Although I had visited Belize before, I realized there were things I hadn't noticed the first time around.

We painted a preschool, one that could have been my own son's in Kentucky. There were 12 of us painting with one roller, a few old brushes, and cups dug out of the trash. We used children's safety scissors to open two old cans of paint, and when we ran out of green paint, I went into town to search for more. I arrived back at the preschool with a color that was 'close enough' and we all laughed about how that would not fly in the States.

Sitting on the tarmac, I realized what I had learned and subsequently taken from my 4-day experience abroad. As a driven professional, known to scare student workers with my level of intensity, I thought to challenge myself with a new personal motto: *close enough*. I found a sense of freedom in the Belizean way of life and sought to redefine my life in a way that wasn't about being perfect and having the best.

Knowledge acquired by successfully managing students outside a traditional classroom, or effectively managing a crisis abroad, can enhance your self-confidence, professional worth, and job marketability. If and when the time is ever right for you to move to a new institution, you will have a step above the rest. Think about it: when you lead a group abroad you become interpreter, facilitator, cheerleader, route finder, food gatherer, disciplinarian, troubleshooter, and problem solver. Leading a study abroad program is the ultimate challenge in multi-tasking. You gain not only cultural knowledge but the keen ability to juggle the many, simultaneous demands of guiding students through their international education pursuits.

Professional advancement opportunities may also be enhanced by leading programs abroad. The movement across higher education to internationalize curricula is inescapable. Integrating your study abroad program into the curriculum, and enabling students to earn valuable credit toward their degree, will only strengthen your future academic opportunities. If you would like to break into the administrative and leadership side of higher education, managing a study abroad experience is a fitting path. There are few academic fields left untouched by international study. Having created and led a program abroad will help you advance and perhaps ensure your place at a larger table of discussion.

My wife and I have international MA degrees and wanted to be abroad. However, at one point we found ourselves in business-related careers that were very unsatisfying. We decided to chuck it all and join the Peace Corps, thinking it would help us later to pursue careers with the Department of State, the CIA, or USAID. While doing our Peace Corps service in Ukraine, we worked with various universities and began to see the limitless opportunity for study and service-learning programs. Sadly, we also saw the extremely poor quality of faculty-led programs that were operated not only in Ukraine but throughout Eastern Europe. There were many shocking lessons in what *not* to do, as well as many lost opportunities for cross-cultural learning, friendship building, and sustainability, not to mention a reckless disregard for adequate health and safety measures. My Peace Corps service and the experience of not just visiting a country but living there, fitting in, and competently adapting, brought me to my current role of developing and leading a variety of programs abroad, as well as training others to do this properly.

While some may plan to be lifers at one institution, it is also likely that many will seek advancement opportunities elsewhere. If you are in a field or on a campus where student participation in study abroad is low or not a priority, don't allow this to stop you. If you cannot find enough interested students at home, you can work cooperatively with faculty from other institutions to recruit, or you can market your program nationally. No matter the field and no matter the institution, international activity speaks for you on a resume and in an interview. Working cooperatively with another institution or two or three may speak even louder. If you are looking for a tenured position, you will surely find that international activity helps.

It's never too late to go abroad. As a matter of fact, many faculty choose to teach abroad *because* they did not study abroad as a student. Others teach abroad because they lived abroad as a child or come from other nations and cultures. The reasons are many and varied, but the benefits are undeniable no matter who you are or what kind of academic background or preparation you have in international travel and teaching.

1.3 For Love or Money

Does your university value international education? If university incentives are not in place to reward you for your considerable work toward leading a study abroad program, then you'll have to think carefully about whether it's worth your time and effort. If you have a young family, or are caring for elderly parents, it may be difficult for you to get away. This is a personal decision that only you can make, depending on your values, where you want life to take you, and what you are willing to sacrifice in order to get there.

Incentives come in many shapes and sizes, and don't always have immediate monetary value. Study abroad leadership will likely help your tenure and review process. Some institutions categorize international activities separately while others consider them within the established teaching, research, and service categories. If this is the case, faculty may be able to use international education across multiple categories by parlaying, for example, an international teaching experience into a journal article or committee work.

> International activity was a big part of my tenure and promotion processes and has been an important part of my teaching, research, and service loads for several years. More recently, as I was pondering an opportunity to move to another institution, my involvement with international education became a factor in my university's endeavor to keep me.

When compensation is lacking, it may be possible to negotiate release time for the course you teach on a study abroad program. Faculty from many different institutions have successfully negotiated release time through study abroad teaching arrangements. Even if this has not been a pattern in your department, or at your institution, it's worth a try. Someone has to go first. Be flexible and approach your Department Chair with an open mind and multiple options. It could very well be that he or she supports faculty-led study abroad, but hasn't seen interest from within the department.

Universities that use release time to support study abroad ultimately result in lower student costs since faculty stipends do not need to be calculated into the program fees. If your university charges home tuition to students on top of program costs, you should advocate for faculty to be paid by the university and not the program. Your institution may run into ethical challenges if you charge students both tuition and include faculty compensation in the program fee. Charging students full home tuition and/or fees when they are not enjoying the benefits of those charges is another topic of debate. While credit warrants a fee, it does not warrant full tuition if the program is self-supporting.

Don't assume your university will fit into one category or another, check with your study abroad office. Some universities pay full 'additional' salary, others provide course releases, others pay a stipend of some kind, and still others pay nothing at all. Most universities will have a method for covering your expenses, such as airfare, on-site transportation, housing, and per diem on top of whatever they deem as compensation. However, be sure to ask! Never assume anything in study abroad, as every university does it differently.

No matter what kind of compensation is offered, try to see the other benefits of leading a study abroad program before you make your decision. We encourage students to do unpaid internships, knowing that *experience* opens doors and leads to other great opportunities. Yet, there's a tendency for us to think we know it all, and therefore, are too valuable to work for free. Such pride has a way of shooting people in the foot, so be careful.

Expenses

If you are dealing with a system in which no incentives are offered, then at the very least, your expenses should be figured into the student cost of the program. This should include everything from the recruiting pizza party to the fliers, mileage for driving to the airport, your flight, every activity abroad, your meals, housing, and the trip back home. You should not be expected to spend your own money. If you are creating the budget, then you have the ability to figure in these necessary program expenses. If your students are not charged university tuition, these items can be figured into the tuition category for student financial aid purposes. You are not cheating the students. Without you, the students wouldn't have a program option to participate. Just as students know their university tuition pays the salaries of the faculty who teach them on campus, they also expect to pay the faculty who teach them abroad.

If you cannot afford to teach abroad without compensation for doing so, you should check with your study abroad office to find out if your university belongs to any consortia. Teaching through a consortium often pays a stipend and covers program expenses. This may give you the peace of mind you need to turn down the paid summer teaching job at home in favor of teaching abroad.

Family

What about taking your family with you on a study abroad program? Check with your university regarding policy and procedure. When permitted, it is definitely a nice perk for faculty who lead programs abroad. However, it is not recommended for the first time. Get your feet wet and a realistic sense of the energy and effort it takes to direct the program before you engage the family. Then, for the next go around, you will be able to give your family an accurate view of the experience and the amount of time you will need to spend away from them with the group. You should always take a second adult to watch over a child under the age of sixteen. There are many reasons for this, one being if your child becomes ill, another adult can provide care.

> My wife and I jointly lead a service-learning program abroad every summer. Operating together makes things much more enjoyable. We each have a share of the responsibilities and know when the other needs down-time.

Over the years, we have seen more desire from faculty with young families to lead study abroad programs, and we encourage them to consider short-term programs abroad. There are ample opportunities to teach abroad long-term. In fact, faculty leaders take their entire families with young children for semesters at a time. However, there are even more opportunities to teach abroad on short-term programs—one to three weeks—with or without the family. A short-term program is more appealing if you have young children or ailing parents that require your attention. It can give you a needed break, or if you want to take your family along, you have the opportunity to plug them into a structure without stealing them away from school, activities, or other obligations for an extended period of time.

> Leading programs abroad with a young family hasn't been much of an issue for me. My son knows that mommy travels for work and respects it. Before a trip, his father and I always teach him about the place where I'll be going, and while I'm gone we have special ways to include him in the program as well. His father talks to him nightly about where I am on the globe and what I am doing there, and I send emails and postcards every day to tell him what I did that day which reminded me of him.

Is it a Vacation?

It is sometimes difficult to help others see the many opportunities in teaching abroad. It is not a vacation, even though as faculty leaders you get to see amazing sites and view the world. The difference between study abroad and a vacation is not only the credit; it is the challenge. You are teaching while managing a group of college students who may or may not think they need managing. You handle crises and answer the calls of university officials and parents. Your success abroad is made on your ability to multi-task so that the sick student is cared for at the same time that a tour is going on for the other 19 students. It is not a vacation and bringing your family into the organized chaos that study abroad can sometimes be should not be taken lightly. If they come along, your family should understand that students have priority if there is a midnight call or a crisis to be managed.

1.4 Without You, Students Will Not Go

You, the faculty, are the number one recruiter for study abroad. Your study abroad office can visit every single classroom, hold study abroad fairs, create advertising materials for you, build a web page, get you on Facebook, hang posters and fliers all over campus, and list your program in national directories, but without you talking to students about international education it will never succeed. Students trust you. Parents trust you. And when you tell them about study abroad, they listen.

Do you have first-generation college students? First-generation students (and their parents) need faculty-led programs. They are much more comfortable with one of their own faculty and often will not even consider independent or direct-enroll programs at a university abroad. They need the comfort of a friend, a faculty, or a staff member from your institution. Parents also feel at ease knowing someone is there to lead the way and help with any problems that might occur. Don't underestimate your program as the only path for many of your students to study abroad.

The students who hear you talk about study abroad may have never considered the possibility. With you teaching a course that they need, their minds open. You talk to them about cost, guide them through the application process, and they suddenly have a cheerleader. And then, there are the students who do not go with you in the summer, but start saving for a future opportunity. You may not even know you are reaching those students, but you planted a seed when they heard you talk about your program. You are the front line and the driving force for study abroad to thrive at your university. If you don't do it, who will?

1.5 University Advancement

Is your university trying to delve into international education but hasn't figured out how exactly to go about it? Many small institutions do not have study abroad offices, and so providing incentives for study abroad programs simply hasn't been addressed. This presents a unique opportunity for you to lead the way. There may also be international activities in place that you don't know about, such as the publicizing of international accomplishments or an international honors society you may be able to join. Find out where your university falls on the internationalization scale and move it forward. If you find yourself spearheading several efforts to systematize international activities on your campus, you're probably building your reputation on that platform. It may be discouraging if others do not share your enthusiasm and drive, but keep pushing forward and appreciate every small step and international education victory.

If your university has a mission to internationalize, whatever their definition, it must include study abroad. You contribute to the greater mission by teaching abroad. In turn that helps bring students to the university. Those whose role it is to participate in high school recruitment days or meet with prospective students will find themselves discussing study abroad with these students and parents, perhaps sharing information about your program, showing that your university does not pay lip-service to globalization but does something about it. We are all ambassadors for our institutions, both positive and negative.

Laura, a prospective student, came to see me with her mother when trying to decide where to attend college. She had been offered the highest scholarship possible at our institution, a public university, and had several offers on the table from other private and public schools in the state. Laura sat on my couch with her mother for over an hour as we chatted about how she could be involved with international studies while on campus. We delved into my personal experiences as an undergraduate at the same institution, my study abroad experience and eventual work abroad. I was able to convey to Laura the importance of study abroad at our institution, point out the specific programs that would work for her intended field of study, and where she could go with a degree from here. Laura later told me that she walked out of my office sure that this was the place for her.

While you are abroad, you may find yourself meeting international students who are interested in studying at your institution. If this is the case, your program is also a vehicle for recruiting international students. Since you've already made the university-to-university connection in building your program abroad, why not host a recruiting even while you're there? You may extend your cooperation into an exchange agreement and/or generate a regular flow of international students from that institution. More than helping your students go abroad, you can contribute to the education of international students and domestic students on your campus. The perspective of the international student in the domestic classroom is priceless for the 95% of American college students who will never get on a plane to study abroad.

Unfortunately, many institutions do not actively support study abroad programs, for various reasons. On many campuses international education is defined solely in terms of recruiting international students. If this is the case on your campus, don't be discouraged; instead, help your institutional colleagues see how study abroad can advance their goals. Your international experience is of great benefit to you and your students. The administration will catch up eventually.

Bringing it Home

When you are challenged to teach in a new and exciting way, you will likely find that excitement spilling back into campus. We all face slumps in our careers. Teaching abroad can reinvigorate your spirit. Experiencing challenges and figuring out how to teach the content from a different landscape gives you a new toolbox to design your courses at home. Infusing an international perspective into any course that has grown weary will *wake up* its content and make it exciting again for you and your students. You become a better teacher after teaching abroad, and incorporating your international experience into courses back home may be easier than you think. Though class time is precious and your syllabus is packed full, there are many possibilities.

An experienced faculty-led program director gave her standard composition course an international theme and paired it with a studio art course taught by another experienced director. Art students choose a geographic area that the composition students use as their focus for writing projects throughout the semester. Composition students provide a copy of their papers to the art students, who create a print, based on each paper's theme. What a great way to expose students to international ideals—all from two instructors who spent time abroad yet came to know very quickly that no matter the value of study abroad, not every student will have the opportunity.

Study abroad veterans will also come back to the home campus and take part in your classes. You will find them contributing to the internationalization of your classroom through broader views and ideals. And you will also find them seeking out the values, ideas, and opinions of international students when they might not have done so before. The students in your classes who will never study abroad can then benefit from the global ideals being shared and debated, in a space where these ideals may not have been available before. They hear international perspectives from their peers, see international students included in conversations, and become more accepting and open.

We often use our subject area as an excuse to shrug off internationalization. How can someone in more factual and rigid academic programs alter course curricula to integrate global ideals? A mathematics professor taught abroad for decades in England. The landscape of Newton and theory behind the solution was the focus of his course. He used what he learned abroad to alter his normal lecture to include discussion and practice in a way that he never done before. The professor learned to think outside the box. This is exactly what we want our students to do, too.

Committee Work

After teaching abroad you may become involved in the international committee structure at your institution or help create one if it is not pre-existing. Find out what exists and see how you can be involved. You may find an extensive structure to support study abroad, international students, international campus programming, and international faculty and staff development. You may also be able to help with study abroad or international student scholarship selection; international teaching applications or international research grant selection; or help with international forums, panels, and performances. Serving on these committees will give you the opportunity to fulfill obligations for your tenure and promotion, while creating new opportunities for students and faculty, as well as solidifying policy.

If no international committees or systems exist at your institution, then create one. Or, spearhead an effort that will encourage and drum up support. Providing a structure for existing international programs, ideas, and dueling missions will help to organize efforts and ensure that you are not competing with each other. It will also encourage onward movement toward a common set of goals. Proper program development and collaboration of like-minded colleagues will go far in this creation, even if you are starting at ground zero. We all had to start somewhere, and one person had to take the lead.

In addition to the international committee structure that may be available for you to serve on, think about the current university committees you are already involved with. Infusing international goals into a university budget committee may help find more funding for study abroad scholarships or faculty stipend support for those who teach abroad. Bringing your international experience to the university general curriculum committee may result in an 'international' category in the core curriculum for all students. You can and will bring your international perspective with you, wherever you go.

Grant Work

International linkages written into grant proposals can result in greater funding opportunities for you, your department, and your institution. Faculty in the sciences are keenly aware of the necessity to seek and secure outside funding for research and expansion opportunities. Your international experience as a backdrop for new grant proposals can help to find new possibilities within the invited grant structure. A corporation seeking to support educational opportunities for women in the STEM (Science, Technology, Engineering, and Math) fields may look very favorably on a proposal that incorporates a study abroad scholarship or research opportunity abroad. Including that international component may be the impetus you need to push your proposal to the funding finish line. Finding ways to expand your grant ideas into international developments and partnerships can help you secure funding, but can also promote research expansion, service, and if you dare, publications.

Project Development

Many faculty take on projects before they realize what they have done. It all starts with a bright idea at a faculty meeting before spiraling into what begins to feel like an additional career path. Projects can take on many forms: rewriting policy, compiling data, event-planning, hosting individuals and groups, entertaining potential hires, advising prospective students, and much more. Projects can take up much of our time and energy, so we should do everything we can to make sure they're interesting. By infusing an international component into a project, we showcase its importance, not only to us but to our department and campus as well. We carry the torch of internationalization and keep our own interests moving forward in international education. For example, you may be in charge of scheduling interviews for new faculty candidates, and arranging a meeting with your study abroad official suggests that international education is important to the department. By including international students in an open interview forum with your candidates, you learn about their cross-cultural communication skills, and demonstrate the importance of your international student body.

Internationalization

Internationalization is the buzzword of the decade. If your university has not already spent considerable time, energy, and funding on efforts to be more accessible to international students, support study abroad, increase the international mobility of faculty, and infuse international content into the curriculum, then just wait, the day is sure to come. You can either start the wave, ride it, or be knocked down when it hits.

With the current economic climate, universities are being challenged just to maintain, much less increase, enrollments. We are constantly reinventing ourselves with new, global-minded tag lines and strategic goals. As a faculty member, you will be expected to contribute to the global goals of the university in addition to local enrollment. How does your academic department, and university at large, attract high caliber, open-minded students? Prospective students are not looking for the prettiest campus or the newest dormitory, or even the university that offers the best scholarship package. In the past 10 years, conversations with prospective students have evolved from 'what is study abroad' to 'how will this help me in my chosen major.' Students come to your campus ready to seek out international opportunities. If you cannot deliver, your elite students will be drawn elsewhere. The fact that study abroad has come to be a required component of many Honors programs is no coincidence. Exceptional students are not scared away by study abroad, but instead attracted to a university that promotes international activity. Students of this caliber already know that having international experience on their resume will push them further up the ladder and offer more opportunities for success in their field.

Given the push and pull of universities experiencing budget cuts, furloughs, larger classes, and decreased benefits, how can we stay on track with greater academic and co-curricular goals? Regardless of cost, globalization is what will move your campus forward. Stay the path and continue to offer study abroad programs that excite you, your students, and your faculty colleagues. Then bring those experiences home to contribute to recruitment, service, and publications. Don't underestimate the fact that one experience can snowball into a varied career path and expanded curriculum vitae that puts you in the middle of internationalization efforts on your campus.

1.6 The Last Word

No matter where you are in your career or where your institution is in its efforts to globalize, study abroad can help your personal, professional, and institutional advancement. Even if there are no resources for a study abroad office, or processes for developing faculty-led programs, you can still lead students abroad. This book will assist you to create the processes for those that come behind you. Yes, it will require some work. Yes, it will be difficult.

Yes, you may have to fight to convince others of the need on campus. But remember, the reward will far outweigh the sacrifice, and you will have helped change many lives in the process.

Chapter Two: From Concept to Reality

So it's time to turn your idea into a program. No doubt, this is the fun part, but don't underestimate the depth and quantity of items to consider in this process. And don't be mistaken, depending upon your experience, it can be a tad bit overwhelming. Look on the bright side; you're already halfway there! By taking time to read this book, and do things the right way, you're being *proactive* and saving yourself the trouble that comes from hasty and imprudent decisions.

As you're going through the planning and implementation process, remind yourself that creating a study abroad program is similar to other types of research and development; there are crucial steps to follow, requirements to fulfill, budgets to maintain, deadlines to meet, and people to please. The more effort you devote to this process, the better your program will turn out, and the greater your reward will be when it's all said and done. By giving yourself plenty of time for planning, you will be able to develop and execute a first-rate, sustainable program.

2.1 Which came first—the course or the location?

Do you know more about your course than the location? Or, do you know more about the location and wonder if you can conjure up a course that fits? This section will help you connect the two, and guide you through other such early and vital decisions.

Your study abroad course should be so integrated with the location that it cannot be executed anywhere else. It should facilitate comparative study within your field, and reflect the city, country, culture, significant people and sites, foreign language, and more. You cannot teach a complete study abroad chemistry course in Japan without visiting local chemistry labs and introducing your students to a comparative study of chemistry in the country. This is crucial! Do not create your course without the country or your country without the course. Marry them and make them one.

Case Study

Two study abroad proposals were submitted by two different faculty members in the same department. The committee knew the student pool was not large enough to support two programs and thus recommended only one proposal be accepted.

- What selection criteria might a university employ in the decision-making process? How can you make sure that your proposal meets or exceeds the criteria, so that your program is approved?
- If both proposals were equally strong, what might be the process to determine which to approve? Is the department Chair involved? Are faculty granted approvals for alternating years? Or, could the faculty combine their efforts?

What makes or breaks a true faculty-led program is the connection between the course and the location. If students can state on their evaluation form that the course could have been taught somewhere else in the world, then you have failed in planning. You did not create a study abroad program, but rather a *tourist adventure*. The course-location combination is what makes the program successful. If you remove the course from the location, it should not succeed; this is how interdependent the relationship needs to be in successful programming.

It's difficult to tie your course to a location when you don't really *know* the location. Before deciding how you will develop your program, it's important to acknowledge your limitations. Maybe you visited, once, ten years ago while on vacation. Or perhaps you lived there a long time ago. Changes can and do occur, and the cost, hot spots, and safe havens of a place you once knew may no longer be the same. If developing the program through your own knowledge and expertise, at least one faculty leader (developer) should have recent firsthand experience in the host country.

Make a list of program logistics that you and your co-leaders can organize, given your past experience and current knowledge of the location. What can you do from your phone and email in the US? What can you do once you are on-site? Consider all components needed to make a program successful: housing, excursions, on-site transportation, local support for health-safety and crisis management, and language fluency. Now, do you really know enough to develop a quality program there, or could you use help from the experts in the study abroad office or a travel company?

It's also important to understand your university policies. If you have a centralized study abroad operation that requires program proposals to be submitted and reviewed for official approval, then there may be a stipulation addressing faculty leader's experience in the location abroad. If it is required that one or more leaders have visited the location, and you have not, inquire about grant funding. Program development grants may be available through your study abroad office, university, or educational consortium. You may also consider a professional development program in the target location. If your university does not offer such programs, take a look at FacultyAbroad.com.

2.2 Making Contacts Abroad

It would be ideal if we all had a best friend living exactly where we want to take students. It would be even better if that friend was also a physician and his spouse a multi-lingual tour guide. How convenient it would then be to organize housing, excursions, and plan for student health emergencies over a single phone call. But this isn't realistic, and unless you are originally from that country yourself, or recently lived there for an extended period, you probably won't have a best friend there either. Here are a few options to locate people with in-country experience.

Study Abroad Office

The study abroad office should be your first stop. The staff will either assist you with personal knowledge of the international site or connect you with an organization, institution, or company that can help pull your program together, by providing the level of logistical support you need.

Education USA (www.educationusa.info)

Education USA is a US government network of more than 400 international advising centers originally set up to offer comprehensive information about educational opportunities in the US. This network has recently opened its knowledge and expertise (free of charge) to study abroad professionals and faculty in the US looking to develop programs in their host countries. Start by contacting one of 14 Regional Educational Advising Coordinators (REACs) who oversee the different countries and provide logistical support and training for the advisers in their regions. Alternatively, contact the country director yourself through the "Find an Advising Center" tool online.

Faculty

Does your university have a database of faculty expertise or an international committee structure built of faculty? If so, use them to find your colleagues who have experience in the target location. If not, then ask around. Find, or create, a list of faculty and staff who have Fulbright, Rotary, and/or Peace Corps experience. Inquire about sending a campus announcement or email questionnaire to faculty. Find out who has been where and see if they can help. Your study abroad office should have a list of faculty and staff who have led programs abroad, and your international admissions office probably has information on international faculty. Finally, find out if there are guest professors on campus from your target country.

US Embassy

You may receive on-site assistance from embassy personnel not only in making local business or university contacts, but also in learning invaluable information concerning possible health and safety issues. Much will depend on whom you happen to reach at the embassy but it's worth a try. Check the Department of State directory of Embassies, Consulates, and Diplomatic Missions online (www.usembassy.gov) and go directly to these websites to gather detailed information.

> I was assisted by a US Embassy staffer in finding a reputable taxi service and online tour company in Ukraine. In a country notorious for financial scams, it was a relief someone could suggest a trustworthy company that I could work with online, from the US, and make credit card payments without worry of identity theft.

Overseas Security Advisory Council (OSAC)

OSAC is a Federal Advisory Committee with a US Government Charter to promote security cooperation between US interests worldwide and the Department of State. This is an excellent free resource for on-site safety information. OSAC staffers will gladly answer your email or phone calls regarding questions you have on areas of the city, safe travel in the country, and what to avoid. Your institution can also join OSAC for free at www.osac.gov, and become a constituent to access exclusive content.

> For a program in Belize, we could save several thousand dollars by flying students into Cancun and driving across the border to Corozal, where the program was situated. I called OSAC's Mexico desk to ask about the safety of driving across the border and received prompt and personal service—an actual human being answered the phone on the first call!

Target-Country Embassy in the US

Typically, the staff at foreign embassies will send you packets of tourist information that you can use to get started. They may also be able to provide you with detailed local information to help with planning, but it depends on the country and the individual you speak with on any given day. I have been rudely transferred from one person to another by one Consulate-General office, but treated to more extensive information than I requested at another. You never know what you will get but it is worth your efforts to attempt these contacts.

Peace Corps Volunteers (PCV) and Returned Peace Corps Volunteers (RPCV)

Who better to give you first-hand information than those who have lived on-site? PCVs and RPCVs, by the very fact that they are or were typically on their own in a city or village for an extended period, know the location very well. If you are looking for housing, ideas for excursions, interpreting services, universities or schools to work with, and more, finding a PCV or RPCV to correspond with could probably help. Another good resource is the Peace Corps Coverdell World Wise Schools Program, which is a correspondence program that matches you to a current volunteer. This is a great way to get to know the country or region for you and your students. The program offers handbooks and classroom guides to educators as well. For more information, visit www.peacecorps.gov/wws.

SECUSS-L

This large listserv was created by study abroad professionals as a communication device for anyone in the field. Given that thousands of professionals read SECUSS-L messages daily, it is a nice place to ask about everything from program provider reviews to available housing in Rome. We have asked many questions ranging from third-party providers to assessment to scholarship policies and more, receiving up to 50 responses each time. You can join yourself or ask your study abroad office for assistance.

Students

You may already have international exchange or degree-seeking students on your campus from the target country. Check with your international student services office. If they can connect you with international students, you may soon find that you have unrestricted access to natives in the target location. When international students are thankful for their experiences, and people who have helped them, they are usually more than willing to help us make contacts abroad.

> A student from Poland participated in a program that houses international students with local families during university and holiday breaks. The student was placed with a faculty member who teaches on campus. That initial weekend experience turned into a full-time homestay, followed by a study abroad program in Poland the next summer.

You may also meet US students who have lived or studied in the target country. They can be invaluable in making contacts, but also in providing a US perspective on transportation, housing, and activity/excursion ideas. Educators can often downplay the input that students provide because *we* are here to teach *them*. Don't underestimate the amount of relevant and useful information you can glean from the student body.

> On our campus, we have a large number of students who grew up in Malaysia and some African countries as the children of missionaries. Their insight and experiences have been invaluable in setting up opportunities for study and research in those same locations. Additionally, the assistance they provide in making phone calls or sending emails in the native language has saved us much time and frustration.

2.3 Program Development Options

There are three ways to create a faculty-led program from start to finish. Each comes with its pros and cons and offers a different degree of ownership over the experience. While outsourcing to a reliable third party can cost more than doing everything on your own, it usually results in better service and shifts liability away from you and your institution. Start with your study abroad office and check the deadline for new program proposals since many universities have deadlines twelve to eighteen months in advance.

Then, talk the idea over with study abroad professionals who can assist you in making proper decisions for your program.

DIY: Do It Yourself
If you decide to DIY, you must be decisive and willing to stand by your work. Everything sinks or swims based on the decisions you make. As such, you should document and support all of your program decisions. You must ensure that your program is academically relevant, that the location and the course are intricately intertwined. If international programs are assessed for global competencies, then your goals must be clear and your planning must reflect those goals. You must ensure that all coursework, excursions, modes of transportation, and especially the location not only relate to each other but are also fused together.

Before you do it yourself, be sure you know the regulations and expectations established by your university, and managed by the study abroad office. It's especially important to understand your responsibility and what sort of training is offered or required for faculty leading programs abroad. If some sort of faculty training for study abroad program leaders is required, then be thankful and appreciative. Faculty training usually also comes with strong support mechanisms prior to departure and while abroad. Training will provide you with information on risk, students, responsibility, how to prepare, and how to respond to crisis.

Pros: You will have control over every aspect of your program, from housing to excursions, flight options to meals, and overall cost. Going it alone from start to finish ensures that the experience is your creation. The students will see, learn, and do exactly what you have planned for them. They may be as pampered or as independent as you like. Everything flows from you. If planned and carried out properly, this program development and implementation experience adds a notch to your belt.

Cons: Having control requires a great deal of time and energy to plan properly. If you cannot balance your checkbook, learn now because you will be held accountable for spending. If your university does not offer training for faculty leading programs abroad, you will be going it alone, so be sure to read this entire book. Chapter 3 covers many aspects of faculty training, and important things you will need to know.

Collaboration with a Third-Party Provider

The process of choosing a third-party provider is an important one. Multiple factors must be weighed, including your preference for a US or host-national company. Before you go hunting, check with your study abroad office. Your university may already work with third-party providers capable of building faculty-led (commonly known as 'customized') study abroad programs. It may also be that your university restricts the use of new providers, especially when going to locations offered by a current affiliate. If you are not restricted, check the Customized Program Provider Directory on Facultyled.com, where you can search more than 50 providers by keyword, location, services, and specialty. Some third-party providers will even advertise your program across their constituency, to help with recruitment. This may or may not be appealing to you, so clarify your market in the beginning.

Pros: Third-party providers have access to housing, classrooms, and local staff, and they usually have a number of resources to draw upon for occasional lectures or even full courses. As such, you are not required to have extensive local knowledge. Typically, you submit your ideas and a proposed itinerary. Then, the provider reviews and responds to you with more details and prices. This becomes the starting point for discussion, feedback, and negotiation. A service contract is later signed between the provider and your university. It simplifies planning, as the provider usually assumes responsibility for all logistical arrangements, except international transportation, and sometimes even more.

Cons: Third-party providers cannot offer their services for free, so they add a profit margin to their original cost. This means that if the bus is costing them $100 per person, then they'll be charging you between $130 and $140 per person. Depending on how much they arrange, the program can get rather pricey for students. If you work at an institution with low tuition rates, and students who are dependent on financial aid, this could be problematic. If your institution adds tuition on top of the program fee, then it may not attract students, especially if there are other more cost-effective programs available through your university. Start the process early to determine if the price is competitive or not.

Additionally, if your institution restricts you to its current affiliates, you may face a geographic limitation unless the third-party provider is willing to expand to a new location. If you are not able to choose a provider on your own, this could be time-consuming and frustrating. Ask your study abroad office for guidance or seek advice externally if resources are available to you. If not, consider the following tips on how to select the right third-party provider.

How to select the right Third-Party Provider
• Request bids from several companies. The negotiating you do will usually surface at least one shining star.
• What is included in the estimated cost across your bids? Be sure to compare apples to apples.
• How flexible is the third-party provider with program dates?
• Can the company customize a program for you or will your group join another group (catalog program) on site? Which do you prefer? How quickly can the company get a customized add-on to you if desired?
• Will the company provide a tour guide and/or translator on the ground? If not, do you really need one?
• Are deposits required? How flexible are payment dates? Can students utilize federal and state financial aid?
• What is the minimum participation needed to cover the cost

of one faculty member? Two faculty members?
- Are there any age minimums, maximums, or changes in the fee structure according to age?

Collaboration with Host Entities Abroad

Check with your study abroad office and find out if your institution has any exchange or other partnerships with universities in the target location. Even if you already know that your university has an agreement in a location, it is important to work together with the study abroad office to determine if others on your campus are already operating faculty-led programs and utilizing the spirit of the international partnership to the extent that fits the university's goals. It is critical that you keep any current efforts centralized and not jump ahead by contacting a university partner directly without proper authorization.

> Everything is negotiable. On one summer program in Ukraine, we received a substantial discount on housing in exchange for lectures in English to local students at the partner institution. This was not a bad trade-off for just a few hours per week.

You are not limited to universities either. Faculty have worked with NGOs, local schools, learning institutes, foreign language schools, expatriates, government entities, field stations, etc. The possibilities are endless.

Pros: If your institution is receiving international students from an exchange partner abroad, and has not been sending domestic students to balance the exchange, your program may be a good solution to correct the flow of students, and enable the exchange agreement to continue. Working with a *university* abroad can give you access to local faculty for lectures or language instruction. If your program assists with a balance issue, a number of other free benefits may also emerge, such as classroom space, dormitory rooms, meals, airport transfers, local transport, activities and tours, and translation services. Even if you are not balancing an exchange, you may still receive these services at a discount, in the spirit of the partnership.

> Two long-standing faculty-led summer programs were developed through the framework of existing exchanges that carried an imbalance. Taking US students abroad to the site, where they were housed, fed, provided with local language lessons, and led on excursions by the institution allowed a mutually beneficial relationship to blossom—one which fostered a discussion on new opportunities to further expand cooperating ventures.

Cons: Curfews, lack of air conditioning, and other inconveniences may frustrate your traditional college-aged students. The university location may be far away from the city limits, resulting in a lengthy trek to get where your students will undoubtedly go often for exploration, shopping, and nightlife. These programs can also be extremely busy with sometimes 'too many' activities, catered by over-indulgent exchange partners. Too much activity can wear on students who need personal time to process the experience and free time to explore on their own. Get details and requirements in advance, including the itinerary and schedule of events, to allow for discussion and negotiation.

Study Tours

Study tours are provided by tour companies. They have a catalog of ongoing tours, from which you can plug in your group. If you anticipate a small group of students, plugging into a catalog program means that you will become part of a large group once on-site. You may choose to add on customized portions at the beginning or end. These companies provide viable solutions for universities where study abroad is not part of the campus fabric and faculty are unlikely to recruit more than a few students.

Pros: If you are planning a short program between one and three weeks, you can easily work with a tour company to fit your summer, winter, or spring break programs into a pre-planned tour.

They utilize extremely knowledgeable guides and provide all on-site arrangements. It is painless to plan a program like this if your course fits into one of their inexpensive catalog options. If you are not plugging into a large tour, the company can provide a "menu" of services from which to choose: excursions, lectures, housing, transportation, airport transfers, and even meal options.

Liability is shared among multiple parties, decreasing the pressure on any one entity. However, be sure the company you choose carries liability insurance and a license to operate abroad.

Plugging into an existing tour means cost is contained, even with just five students. These tours are usually advertised across the US, so you could end up meeting some interesting people in your tour group, creating diverse and culturally dynamic interaction. These companies typically offer free rides to faculty with a minimum number of participants.

Cons: You probably won't have any choice in the hotels, transportation, and activities built into a catalog tour, and regardless of whether you take advantage of all of them or not, you will still pay the same. If you want to customize a catalog tour with *add-ons*, or changes, it can be rather expensive. Companies that offer these add-on options may push you towards their best "menu" items such as 4-star hotels and tours with no student discounts, greatly increasing cost. If you go this route, you must be willing to negotiate in order to keep the program affordable for your students.

Perhaps one of the biggest drawbacks with tour companies is their lack of flexibility regarding payment. They usually require early deposits that do not match financial aid disbursements on your campus, meaning students are often required to pay the whole bill without their financial aid. By and large, need-based students, and their families, don't have this kind of money on hand. If the program requires an early deposit, check with your study abroad office to see if deposit services are provided. Then, set up an early application deadline so that these deposits can be made. Keep in mind that if the program does not meet its minimum enrollment, the university will lose a portion of the deposit.

Another challenge with tour companies is building in class time to an already jam-packed schedule. If you customize your own program, you can build in whatever time you need with your students. However, plugging into a catalog tour means there will be little time to steal away for lecture and reflection. If your class is taking place on the home campus, and you are using the tour as a supplementary component, or field experience, then it may be okay. On the other hand, if the tour is meant to be an all-inclusive course, check with your study abroad office first, since it may not pass the academic standards at your institution.

Program Development Options		
Option	Pros	Cons
Do it Yourself	Independence, Control, Ownership, Accomplishment, University support ensures success	Time, Financial Responsibility, Lack of university support if no study abroad office
Third-Party Provider	Simplified, No extensive local personal knowledge necessary, Experts handle arrangements	Pricey, Institutional policies may prohibit the right fit, Possible geographic limitations
Host Entity	Balance an exchange, Ease of access to local sites, Discounted logistical provisions, Translation services	Inconveniences for students, Location may be a barrier, Busy schedule with little free time
Study Tour	Established catalog programs, Knowledgeable guides on-site, Inexpensive, Can plug into a larger program OR menu items, Diverse people in group, Fits small groups	Add-ons are expensive, Full price for catalog activities not utilized, Deposit due dates, Little or no existing academic structure, No classroom space or class time

Finally, if you wish to deviate from the tour itinerary, such as taking your students to a museum or adding tickets to the opera, this will add cost to the program fee and you will not be provided with a guide. Hence, it is vital you know the locations and venues, as you will be leading students on your own.

2.4 Faculty-Led Program Models
Below are eight models that you can use to fathom and shape your faculty-led program. By understanding the array of possibilities, you will be able to determine the best model or hybrid to utilize. Whatever model you ultimately choose should reflect not only your personal knowledge but also your program goals.

Stationary
You choose a site and stay there. Of course, this does not preclude some built-in excursions to other places relating to program coursework or outcomes, but it does mean that you maintain a single base of operation where most of the program's daily functions take place. This model is very good for creating in-depth cross-cultural experiences. If students are in one place long enough, it can foster a sense of "second home" and a feeling of "knowing" the culture, as opposed to just "seeing" as a tourist. On longer experiences and even some shorter ones, students are able to escape the honeymoon phase of culture shock and see the country and people in a deeper, more meaningful way.

Faculty can foster the intensity of the cross-cultural experience by organizing activities with locals. This introduces students to the people who inhabit the location but also helps students get to know the location, and where they will reside for the next several weeks or months. As a result, students come home with a more authentic understanding of the country, beyond the superficial knowledge that comes from touring.

If adaptation and intercultural competence (as opposed to merely knowledge) are what your program seeks to develop, there is no better model than stationary. However, be practical about the expectations placed on your students if you are stationary for only a short period of time. The way in which activities and locals are built into the program will make the greatest impact on how much of the country and culture is assimilated by the students.

> I use a stationary model for my summer program, which was developed in collaboration with the English translation department of a Ukrainian university. From day one, our students are paired with their host university counterparts and complete a 3-day orientation together. Within a week, they are close friends and within two, they are spending most of their free time together. By the end of the program there are small multi-national groups taking off to travel together and there are often tears shed when it is time to say goodbye and go home.

Multi-Stop

A multi-stop program starts in one place and ends in another, with various stops along the way. This requires more in terms of logistical planning, but it can give your students a greater overview of the country or region than a stationary program can offer. You can include visits to small villages as well as large cities, and your fast-paced students will never get bored.

On the other hand, transportation costs for a multi-stop program can become prohibitive and put your course out of reach for students. Consult with your study abroad office first on a realistic, competitive price range. When bargaining group rates, you can often secure hotels, transportation, tours, and entrances at a discount. Keep this in mind, and make sure students know that going as part of a group will cost less than going on their own. If the goal of your course is to expose students to a variety of international industry then a multi-stop program is likely the best way to go, unless you build a stationary program in a very large city like London or Tokyo where you will have easy access to multiple industry tours and lectures.

One of the hardest things for a faculty leader to decide is what the students should see and do, as it relates to the course, and what to leave out. There must be balance. When you take your first group abroad, you will surely find that some of the activities didn't go as planned. As such, you will have a better grasp on what is appropriate and not appropriate for the next program. The main issue with a multi-stop program is time. If you have only one or two weeks, it's probably not wise to visit four countries, unless you wish to spend the bulk of your time in transit. You must weigh the benefits of quickly rushing through four countries versus getting to know one country, or even one city, in a more meaningful way.

One program on our campus takes place in four cities over four weeks. Student evaluations mention that each shrine or historic site blends into another and that the whole program is a blur. The very hot climate of the country, and the continual use of non-air-conditioned public transportation for lengthy excursions, makes the program insufferable at times. These conditions and subsequent word-of-mouth complaints from previous participants have undoubtedly contributed to a continual decline in program applications.

Island Program
An island program is one in which a group of students, typically from the same country or institution, travel together and stick together with no structural integration into the location abroad. This is different from an integrated program, where students may be living with local families, enrolled in local language classes, or participating in friendship or other cultural programs. Certainly, the easiest form of housing is hotels, hostels, or university dormitories. Friendship programs with locals can be very difficult to organize, so creating independent group activities as you would on a family vacation, tends to be the norm.

Keeping students together can serve a purpose, in addition to assisting faculty who don't have on-site knowledge or are utilizing a tour provider as opposed to a university contact abroad. If your university is concerned with increasing the number of students who study abroad, then island programs will help. These programs serve first-generation and other college students who have never been out of the country before. An island program can expose students to a vast array of subject matter and whet their appetite to learn more about the world. Students who participate in island programs usually come back with greater confidence and often find ways to study abroad again.

Integrated Program

Integrated programs provide structured and unstructured opportunities for students to experience the culture. Integration goes beyond simply arranging homestays, especially if those homestays are with families or individuals who don't engage students.

One way to instill intercultural learning is to challenge students to communicate in the local language and spend time with local people to discuss relevant issues and expose worldviews. Structured contact forces students to interact in a meaningful way. By providing students with a list of points to cover, or questions to ask, you encourage this sort of cultural exchange.

A student returned from a semester abroad and revealed that her host-family experience was less than ideal. She lived with a single elderly woman who drank excessively and was out at all hours of the night. While it was not bothersome enough for the student to complain on-site, it shocked the study abroad staff. When looking into the situation further, it was discovered that previous students who lived with this woman had the same experiences but never thought to tell anyone about it.

You must also consider the thorough vetting of families or individuals that will house your students. We all want our students to have a good experience living with a host family, but in order to protect your students, and cover yourself and your university from potential legal problems down the road, you should consider a workshop or training for families on what to expect from students. Minimum levels of treatment, privacy, attention, and security are legitimate items to discuss with, and expect from, host families, usually compensated for student care.

If you think you can't have an integrated program because it's too short, think again. In just ten days abroad, you can guide transformation in the lives of your students by challenging them from a new perspective. Students don't always have to be comfortable. If your students are comfortable for the entire program, then they've probably not been challenged enough. Even if your program is hotel-based, you can still create an integrated experience that encourages dialog with locals. Take language acquisition and intercultural learning to a much higher level by structuring local students into the program as translators, mentors, or guides.

Competence-building activities, such as citywide scavenger hunts, are an excellent way to build student confidence in the beginning. The faculty leader of a popular semester program in Europe takes participants to a local bus stop on the second day of the program. After showing them which lines to use, how to read the map, and how their bus tickets work, he requires that they meet him on campus the following morning at a specific time. There may be a few stragglers here and there, but they all eventually surface and local transportation becomes one less worry for the director and one more success for students.

Field Study

A field study provides a hands-on opportunity for students in their disciplines. Archaeological digs and biological research are some examples of field studies. Generally, these are arranged through contacts the faculty leader already has abroad from years of research. Utilizing students to continue that research can lead to breakthroughs and joint publications that take the students and faculty to higher professional levels, making field studies an excellent opportunity.

Recruiting students for field studies is not like recruiting for other study abroad programs. These programs are often designed with more moderate to basic accommodations, cafeteria-style or even campfire dining, and little access to bathroom facilities, as we know them. Field studies are not for the faint-of-heart or the high-maintenance student. They require strict attention to rules and guidelines so that artifacts and research are handled properly. That said, great intercultural learning could take place on a field study if the faculty leaders utilize locals and train students to interact appropriately with the culture. Field studies generally provide less free time for shopping and other personal site seeing. They are often located at remote stations, which lack ease and availability of transportation. As such, field studies are for serious academic students who want practical hands-on experience and the opportunity to uniquely construct their resumes.

If you are considering a field study program for majors in the department, assess your pool of students and budget accordingly. If your department has only twenty majors, it is unrealistic to budget for ten on your program. You can run an excellent field study with as few as four or six students. Keeping the program solely academic, without the perks and five-star accommodations of other short-term programs, will help you keep costs low, even with fewer participants.

Language Immersion
Study abroad programs may include a language-learning component in addition to or part of the main course objectives. Perhaps the expectation for students is to attempt some basic conversational language in the native tongue on a program whose focus is archaeology. Altogether separate, are those programs with language immersion goals and a primary focus to train students in the native tongue throughout the program.

Do not attempt this type of program unless you are a language professor yourself, have fluency in the target language, and/or plan to collaborate with a language instructor either here, abroad, or both. A language immersion program considers the target audience first. Are there already significant affordable study abroad opportunities for intensive Spanish that are available to students? Alternately, are students wait-listed every summer for Spanish programs without enough space?

If you lead a language-intensive program abroad, it is vital to infuse it with cultural learning. This is because language and culture are inseparable, and we can't fully grasp one without the other. By infusing cultural knowledge with language teaching, you foster a better understanding of each. Language faculty may teach intensive language courses abroad while utilizing local language instructors for the culture portion, taught in the native tongue. These programs are some of the most successful because students develop greater intercultural competence, which translates into future academic and career goals.

Internships and Independent Study
Directing study abroad programs does not necessarily mean that *you* have to go abroad. If you have students interested in spending time abroad on a research project, studying a foreign language, completing student teaching, or getting work experience, there are ways to make this happen which don't require you to take a group of students to another country. Thanks to technology, and depending upon the country they are in, we can stay in contact with our students, provide timely feedback on projects, discuss research, and assist in most other needed ways.

You may have spent time abroad doing research at a specific institution or with international faculty with whom you maintain contact. If so, arranging an internship opportunity can be easier than you think. Even former students now living abroad could be a source for exploring possibilities. Start with your contacts and plan outward for student housing and supervision. If you want to grow an internship program for your department, travel may be necessary to finalize program details, supervise students, and/or evaluate. Your department may also adopt the program as a point of pride, allowing for expansion into other travel-research opportunities for faculty members.

If you do not have your own contacts abroad for these opportunities, there are a number of companies specializing in international internship placement. Your study abroad office may have more details. There are advantages and disadvantages that go along with each company, but if you do a good job matching the research interests of you and your students, you may be able to develop a long-standing partnership.

For an internship program to succeed on your campus, there are several things that should be in place. If your department does not have an internship course number already established, you will need to pursue one through your academic approval process. You will also need to inquire about financial aid, and if students can use it for internship programs. If they can use financial aid for internships, then ask your career services office how to keep students enrolled to ensure that their financial aid applies to the credit and cost associated with the program.

Service Learning
International service learning is a strategy that integrates community service with guided instruction and reflection to enrich the learning experience. It seeks to fulfill learning objectives for the participants and practical desires for the host community. Because hands-on experience is usually associated with better job prospects, this type of program may be easier to grow than more traditional study abroad formats.

Service learning programs may require extensive research and contacts abroad, as they involve not only logistical coordination, but also student placements in projects that are suitable to the goals of the course. You may have an opportunity to make contacts and look for projects while you are abroad for a different program or purpose. You may also be able to make contacts at a professional conference or organizational meeting, if it attracts international colleagues.

A two-way service-learning program in Ukraine allows for both Ukrainian university students and US university students to work together on a project that fulfills practicum requirements for their respective majors. US students earning TESL certificates or ESL endorsements teach at a public elementary school and local orphanage. Ukrainian students completing degrees in English translation and interpretation work side-by-side the US students, not only as translators in the classroom, but also as culture partners, language instructors, and excursion guides, which greatly increases their English language skills.

2.5 Academics, Credit and Course Models

Students can learn about the history, culture, and language of a country when the study plan is tied directly to the location of the course. Your study plan should contribute to a deeper learning *experience* in the program abroad than its subject matter. Even if you're teaching the same course abroad that you teach on campus, your study plan should be modified to maximize the use of time spent abroad in a meaningful and thought-provoking way. The course development process is an avenue of discovery, how to best incorporate the location in a comprehensive way.

Some professors are surprised at the many ways in which teaching abroad differs from teaching on the home campus. What is different? Well, everything. In an art appreciation class at home, students will sit in the dark and look at slides. In Paris, students will visit the Musee D'Orsay and the Louvre. Simply put, you have an educational playground to offer your students while abroad. As the faculty leader, it is your responsibility to intermingle the syllabus and the playground.

Case Study

While international students are invited to participate in study abroad programs, institutional policy dictates that a student cannot study abroad in her own home country. This is because there is little to no intercultural language or comparative academic learning, which takes place. A faculty member challenged this policy: "Whether I teach a course here or abroad, it's the same subject matter and credit. Isn't it discriminatory to not allow certain students to take my course just because it's being offered abroad?"

- Do you agree with the policy or the professor? Why?
- How would you handle an international student who wishes to take your course in her home country?

There are many opportunities to connect the syllabus with the location. Architecture students can take a walking tour of any city in the world, viewing the cityscape surrounding them and writing a reflective essay. Engineering students can be challenged daily to find good and bad engineering design in the city. A smart professor will find a way to incorporate even the unexpected and divert student attention away from an unwanted delay or cancellation, to the learning experience at hand.

Above all, faculty leaders must remember that learning does not stop. Seven days a week, 24 hours per day, students are given the opportunity to learn. Create opportunities for students to do so, without hesitation. Challenge students to see beyond themselves and learn how their field is practiced around the world. At home, your course may not include any comparative study. However, when teaching abroad, you cannot responsibly ignore it. Infusion. Infusion. Infusion.

Determining credit hours may be out of your hands if you are teaching a transplant course, one that currently exists on your campus. If you have proposed a new course you may designate credit hours, but the real question is how to translate contact hours into credit for the study program. While the process may vary from institution to institution, there are some guidelines.

If your university requires a minimum number of *contact* hours per credit, then you will need to satisfy this requirement. Contact hours are usually coupled with *study* hours to avoid an accrual of too many credits (without enough reflection time) all at once. For example, if one credit approximates the effort expended in a consecutive period of 12.5 "class time" hours and 25 "study time" hours, then only one credit can be earned in a 40-hr week.

Generally, one credit is earned per week in a faculty-led program. If weekends are incorporated into the structure of the course, then credits may climb to two. For the purposes of study abroad, "contact hours" or "class time" may consist of lectures, course meetings (before, during, or after), museum visits, and organized excursions that engage students with the learning objectives of the course. Study time is not calculated, but would naturally include the rest of the week or "free time" that students have to reflect upon the culturally-rich learning environment.

Combination Course

There are different ways in which you can construct your course. A *combination course* is designed so that a substantial portion of class time is spent in a domestic location, before and/or after the program abroad. This structure allows more credit to be earned with a shorter international experience.

In the case of pre-programmed class meetings, students may be better prepared to leave. They are knowledgeable when they get to the international location, eliminating the need to play catch-up with local politics, tradition, history, etiquette, and more. You may also arrive with a better sense of group dynamics, as well as how to manage slackers, overachievers, troublemakers, etcetera.

Post-program activities provide students with an opportunity to reflect on their international experience. Traditional class meetings, conferencing, and/or project work are all excellent ways for them to reflect deeper on what they learned abroad. If you decide to add a post-program component, it is important to draw out meaning, discuss stereotyping that took place, and deepen student reflection on the experience abroad. Don't focus solely on the academics, but also on those culturally surprising tidbits of learning that students are still pondering. Also, spend some time reviewing and assessing individual student goals.

Web-Based Course
If you are interested in a combination course, but will be recruiting students from satellite campuses nationwide, a web-based course is ideal. This course type is taught online in a pre- and/or post-program combination. First, find out what the requirements and/or restrictions are on your campus for web-based courses, including the cost of registration.

A hybrid *web-based* and *combination* course is utilized in a Costa Rica gap program that offers students a 3-credit hour course. Students read the required text, write several papers, and prepare a presentation all via online learning for a 3-week period. The students then come together at the home campus for a two-day program where they deliver their presentation and take part in lectures and other activities. Following the program abroad, students complete final projects and submit them via email.

Domestic Course with International Component
En lieu of a combination course, you can attach an international component (or field trip) to a domestic course offering, so long as the teaching and learning are intricately tied to the travel abroad.

This model may be integrated with a variety of different terms, including but not limited to:

- **Spring Break** – Students are enrolled for the course during the entire spring semester and everyone in the class goes abroad for spring break.
- **Winter Break** – Students are enrolled for the fall semester and then travel abroad for a two-week period during the December-January holiday.
- **Early Summer** – Students are enrolled for the full spring semester and go abroad for a period immediately following university commencement.

It is possible to have a domestic course that includes both students who will participate in the portion abroad and students who will not. The challenge, then, is for the faculty to determine how to prepare the traveling students adequately without neglecting those who plan to stay home, as well as how to work out the differences in credit.

Split-Term Course
Split-term courses generally overlap terms and are conducted both at home and abroad. Below are a few popular combinations:

- Second-half semester spring course combined with a summer program abroad.
- Second-half semester fall course combined with a winter program abroad followed by a first-half semester spring course.
- Second-half semester fall course combined with a winter program abroad.
- A winter program abroad combined with a first-half semester spring course.

Because the course overlaps terms, special arrangements must be made through the Registrar's Office. If grades are to be turned in after a graduation period, consider how this would affect graduating seniors who would like to participate in your program. Can you issue an 'Incomplete' for the grade? If you do, will this affect graduation eligibility? If it will, then is there a way around it?

> A mass communications web-based course held online meetings prior to gathering for the first time in a pre-designated location. Given the depth of discussion that took place online, prior to meeting, the professor and the students felt like they already knew each other's personalities intimately.

All Abroad Course

Aside from a pre-departure orientation and/or a few preparatory meetings, all academic credit is earned abroad. Usually, the same university credit requirements apply to an all-abroad course as to a combination course.

Provide your students with the reading list well in advance. This gives them the choice, and ultimately the responsibility, to either read the material beforehand or spend their precious time abroad reading at the international dormitory instead of seeing, touching, tasting, and feeling the surrounding culture.

2.6 Course Selection and Collaboration

After deciding on a model, you will need to select or develop your course and syllabus, and structure it with a term, start-end dates, and budget. For final course selection, you can either (a) use a course already on the books at your institution or (b) create a new course specifically for your program abroad.

Transplant Course

A transplant course already exists at your home institution, but the syllabus is altered to fit the location. For example, a course in Journalism and Mass Communication may be altered to focus on British media in London as opposed to US media in Chicagoland. Lectures, events, tours, and assignments would also be structured to provide a comparative study of other world systems.

When renovating a transplant course for use abroad, be sure to follow university or department guidelines for the curriculum, especially for core courses in the curriculum. There may be very little or no room to alter textbooks or the content focus. Generally, upper-level courses are more flexible, but these can also be tricky. It all depends on the field of study.

Unique Course

A unique course is created by you, solely for your study abroad program. Before designing a unique course, consult with your department chair. The course may be attached to a study abroad seminar or topics number, to allow for flexibility in the future. It may also be approved to substitute for some required courses or electives in the curriculum.

If course approval is necessary, be sure to factor this into your timeline. Follow mandatory university guidelines for new course creation. Look out for oversights such as program approval, but no course approval, and vice versa. If more than one committee approves the structural components of programs abroad, then the process may be more complicated and time-consuming.

Course Collaboration

Study abroad courses naturally correspond with interdisciplinary studies. Depending on your location and subject matter, students may benefit from the team approach. Your team may be faculty from other departments at your institution or colleagues from the location abroad. The team approach enables you to recruit from a broader base of students, across academic fields or universities. You may consider cross listing the course in two departments; a student studying politics of East Central Europe could equally benefit from ethnicity studies in the Carpathian Basin. Students receive credit in their field but benefit from the knowledge of the leadership team. It's a win-win situation for all.

2.7 Program Information

In addition to the course, consider the need for your program, target population, and student eligibility. Building a program without adequate attention to crucial market details is setting you up for failure. If your program is not needed, does not fill any sort of requirement for students, is too exclusive, or you do not market it to the right audience, it will be unsuccessful.

Purpose and Need

Your program should benefit both you and your students. There is nothing wrong with integrating your own career goals into a program for your students. However, do not focus on yourself to the detriment of the program. Working through how your new program will differ from other long-standing options available to students is important. The task of articulating its unique purpose and goals should not be taken lightly.

Avoid direct competition in your department and university. Sometimes a department chair must step in to mediate when it's unlikely that all proposed programs will succeed with the limited target population. If there is an existing program in your department, but you want to start a new one, sit down with the department chair and perhaps the faculty leader of the existing program to talk through your ideas and how the program will meet different needs. In the case of two or three programs, you may wish to rotate them every two or three years.

Eligibility

What will determine a student's eligibility to participate in your program? Is your program open to all students or students from a particular major? Both to undergraduate and graduate students? Are there course prerequisites? If your field graduates ten majors per year, but offers several required courses across the curriculum, consider pairing one of those required courses with your program abroad. Offering undergraduate and graduate credit to students on the same program is common practice and should be taken into consideration.

Target Population
Only you know your *intended* target audience, but don't overlook the benefits of your program to students in other majors and minors as well. Most faculty-led programs require a minimum number of participants. Do you need to broaden your audience in order to make this happen? A course listed in social work may also attract students from nursing and pre-medicine. To optimize interchangeability, offer your course as an upper-level elective or requirement and incorporate interdisciplinary content.

Term and Dates
There are many factors to consider when organizing your program abroad. The availability of students, financial aid, summer school overlap, the weather, daylight hours, happenings abroad, the host institution's schedule, and price of airline tickets are all important to mull over before you decide on your term and dates. You should also think about your field; for example, occupational safety and health students often secure summer internships in extremely lucrative positions that pay their university tuition, and then some. As such, it is very unlikely they would study abroad during the *summer*. Finally, how much time do you need abroad for your course to be effective? Consider your program goals.

There are typically four term options:
- Semesters or Trimesters
- Winter (or J-term): 1-4 weeks
- Spring break: 7-12 days
- Summer break: 2 weeks to 3 months

Obviously, the more time you have, the more you can do, and the more money you will spend. First, settle on your ideal length based on course goals. Then, work through a budget to determine an estimated cost to students. Finally, if necessary, start cutting costs by an excursion here, a night there, until you reach a competitive price. While important, pricing the program is not all; you must also ensure that it is academically and interculturally relevant. Don't sell your program short by cutting out vital academic and cultural components just to save some money.

Classroom Facilities

Will you have access to a classroom abroad? Is a traditional classroom necessary to the success of the program? If you do not have access to a classroom, how can you alter your course while maintaining its academic integrity?

Teaching abroad is very different from teaching on campus. It is sometimes described as "teaching in the trenches" because you may be conducting class on a bus or train, in a museum or central square. If you are leading a 2-week program and hold a traditional lecture every morning, your students will be disgruntled and you may be missing the advantages of your location and all it could potentially offer—including guest lecturers, tour leaders, museums, and more.

Your facilities will also play a large role in the assignments you can give to students. Students cannot complete a typed technical review following each theatrical performance when they have no access to a computer lab. They can't do book research without the use of a library. A more common approach is to provide a framework for which students keep a journal about their experiences, what they learn, etc. Students can also work on creative projects that involve photography, video, or community service work. Accepting written assignments upon return is also an option.

Itinerary

Your day-to-day schedule makes up your full program itinerary. In addition to academics, your itinerary should consider the following items.

- **Exhaustion** – A schedule from 8am until 9pm may be okay for a few days, but not for 14 days straight. Students, and you, will grow quite weary of each other, the course, and the location if forced to be together for 13 hours a day throughout the program. Sadly, many faculty-led programs operate this way simply because the faculty member thinks mother-henning the students is the only way to ensure their safety. Carefully consider some free time every day, a free day here and there, or free weekends for programs that go longer than two weeks.

- **Excursion Proximity** – Organize your schedule so that excursions are in close geographic proximity to wherever you are stationed that day, as opposed to traveling out of the area or outside of town on multiple days. Combining trips will save money for everyone and maximize time on site, enabling you to take other visits or build more activities into your program, or simply provide more free time throughout.

- **Debriefing** – Students will see, hear, and experience things that need to be digested. Health studies students who visit a Chinese acupuncturist need time to talk about what was seen. Students should not be left thinking, "That's weird" after a structured visit. It is your job to help them process what they are experiencing. Cramming too many visits into a day, or program, without adequate debrief time will only frustrate everyone.

- **Independence** – Students need time to explore on their own, to build a sense of confidence and independence in their new context. If the entire program travels together to every location, your students will have little to no opportunity to gain self-confidence using the local transportation system. If you order food for the group at every meal, your students do not have the opportunity to navigate the cultural and language differences surrounding them. A proper on-site orientation should provide students with the basic skills necessary to do many important things for themselves.

When building a program itinerary, especially for first-timers, there is a tendency to include every activity under the sun and travel together constantly. The hardest thing to do is to decide what excursion or guest lecture to leave out. We can treat students as kids and do too many things for them. If we do not give them time to decompress on their own, explore and get lost, debrief differences, and gain some sense of self-confidence, we do our students a disservice. Sometimes less can be more.

Transportation

Many faculty leaders build international transportation into the program, as opposed to everyone meeting at the international location. Arranging group flights can be as difficult or as simple as you make it. First, check with your study abroad office to find out if they offer any booking support, and be sure to provide them with all the necessary details, including any students who will not take the group flight. If you find yourself making arrangements, consider one of the following:

- **Travel Agents** – It's easy to use a travel agent, but it can increase the cost. Nonrefundable deposits are becoming more common while group discounts are diminishing. You can also reserve tickets with an agent and have your students call them to book individually. This puts details such as seat requests and frequent flier information out of your hands, and makes program financing easier, so that you and your university are not involved in the collection of funds.

- **Online Booking** – Online booking tends to be the most cost-effective. But you or your university have to make a decision about whether to collect credit card numbers from students, have everyone in the room purchase their own tickets at the same time, or book all of them on your own card and deal with reimbursement later. Your university may also purchase the tickets and then bill student accounts.

- **Rendezvous Time** – Identify a window (specific period) and meeting point in the airport, hotel, or another place at the final destination. You can purchase your flight early and provide each participant with a copy of your itinerary, so that all participants can book the same flights if they choose. If you choose a rendezvous time, be sure to have a copy of each participant's flight itinerary so you can monitor status.

Transportation involves more than international flights. You will need to figure all modes of transportation, and their cost, into the program budget: airport to housing, housing to daily excursions, excursion to excursion, housing to airport, etc. Thoroughly vet transportation providers on site. Obviously, this is more important in some countries than in others. Be less concerned with cost than with the qualifications of drivers and condition of vehicles. Most countries have licensing procedures for drivers. Ensure that the company or individuals you choose to contract with meets host country legal requirements.

Calling taxis on site is only problematic because you cannot take the time to sit down and examine their credentials before riding with them. However, you can contact each taxi company in town, speak with the owners or supervisors, and choose one that you will call when needed. Building a relationship with one company can also ensure that your students are treated well and not taken advantage of should they need to use taxis independently.

If you plan to drive students around while abroad, then check with your study abroad office or University Counsel to determine if a release form exists. The standard university release should address public transportation, but private rental is generally not included. Also, find out about any additional requirements. Do you need to be approved by the university to drive? Does the university need a record of clean driving within a specific period of time? Do you need an international driver's license?

It is important to know that most US auto insurance policies are invalid outside of the country. If you plan to drive while abroad, look into a supplemental short-term policy. Perusing the US Embassy's website should help you to find information on reputable insurance providers. Sit down with your University Counsel to determine what level or extent of coverage you should carry before making a final decision. Also, visit the website of ASIRT: The Association for Safe International Road Travel (Asirt.org).

> At an October 2000 Congressional hearing on 'Safety in Study Abroad,' it was stated that the major cause of student injury or death in overseas programs is traffic accidents. According to the US State Department, road travel is the greatest risk to healthy Americans abroad.
>
> The study abroad community can help ensure the safety of students by careful program and itinerary planning, risk assessment, staff and student preparation, and emergency contingencies.[1]

Coach companies are a great idea for the large group traveling out of the city or within a city where public transportation is not advisable, or widely available, or simply isn't practical in terms of time or money. Check prices to determine if a coach is economical for the group. Coaches are usually comfortable and may have amenities like lavatory, television, video, and sound system. With a coach, you can lecture en route or show a video to enhance the learning experience at the next destination. The only drawback to keeping students busy is that they are watching you or the video instead of the scenery passing by outside.

---

[1] ASIRT, http://asirt.org, 9 Feb 2010

Mass transportation like buses, trains, and subways are friends to study abroad in smaller doses. Try herding a group of 20 onto a London city bus and you will quickly come up with an alternative form of transportation. Using public transportation is a great idea, if you use it wisely. Offering your students the option of meeting you at the location is a great use of time and transit, and instills independence in your students. You will find that students utilize even the 6-8am hours to see and do more things, especially on a 10-day or 2-week program, and therefore greatly appreciate the chance to meet you at the 8am activity instead of coming back to your accommodations to depart as a group.

You might also consider providing a pass for the entire program, to save time from repeatedly buying individual tickets. This saves money and gives you peace of mind when your students are out exploring on their own. They will more than likely have a way to get home if they are provided with a transit pass.

Accommodation
There are many accommodation options to consider: dormitory, homestay, apartment, hotel, field station, hostel, or campground. Each has its own advantages and drawbacks. Carefully weighing the program goals with cost is vital to your decision process.

- **Dormitory** – If your program will draw on the relationship your university has with an institution abroad, then contact the institution about dormitory space and availability during your program. This is an example of when changing program dates can drastically reduce cost. Even if you do not have a relationship with an institution abroad, you may still contact a nearby university or institute to see if space is available.

- **Homestay** – For obvious reasons, a homestay is preferable for language-intensive programs and usually comes with a meal plan. Remember however, that you are responsible for where you house students. If you are not well acquainted with the families, you may not wish to take those risks. Don't just put an ad in the local newspaper and take anyone who comes along. If you are planning to utilize homestays, there will be paperwork, screening visits, family contracts regarding what will be provided to the participants, etc. We recommend utilizing the local contacts of a university to find homestays. Alternately you can conduct a site visit or arrive plenty of time ahead of your students to interview and secure families.

- **Apartment** – Because most faculty-led programs are limited in length, the cost of an apartment is always going to be high compared to other options. However, if there is enough room, the students may choose to split the costs and have a private apartment with access to a kitchen, which will also cut the cost of meals. If you are going to a smaller city or town, an apartment may be your only option. Be flexible, and be ready to pay for more than you actually need, to satisfy minimum time requirements for local leasing.

- **Hotel** – Always research local hotels, another reasonable option depending upon where you go and how long you will be staying. If you are planning to use a hotel, you should absolutely have breakfast included for your students. Once on-site for a few weeks or months, you can develop the contacts and relationships for future homestay families or visit potential apartments for the next year. A Ukraine program has often used hotels in downtown Kyiv, which surprisingly are much less expensive than hostels or homestays.

- **Field Station** – Science programs are likely to utilize field stations. When digs or hands-on science exploration and discovery will be the meat of a program, staying onsite is beneficial and cuts out additional transportation costs for students. The drawback is that such facilities are usually rustic. Lack of electricity, telephones, or hot water are better managed when students anticipate them, rather than discover onsite that they cannot dry their hair or call their parents daily. Be sure to inform participants of these conditions in advance.

- **Hostel** – Hostels are multi-bedded rooms that bring us back to our summer camp days. Inhabitants are paying for the bed, not the room, and bed sheets or pillows may cost extra. Bathroom facilities are also shared. Hostels are inexpensive, but it is better to utilize one with a locker system so that you and your students can lock up valuables when out everyday. Your group will not be the only ones staying in the rooms so what to bring, protecting valuables, and personal security will become important elements of your orientation.

- **Campground** – There may even be campgrounds available nearby with cabins. Campgrounds often have more amenities than field stations and cost about the same as a hostel, but in a less shocking environment for students accustomed to hotels and all that comes with them. Typically, a Google search can provide you with contact information and details.

Whatever your choice for accommodation, be sure that it does not impede the experience of your students. If your students are preoccupied with keeping their belongings safe, or wishing they could take a shower, their experience may be hampered. It therefore becomes extremely important for transparent and accurate orientation. Students should know what you know and be prepared for the housing situation, whatever it may bring.

Meals
Meals for the program can be configured in a few different ways. The main thing to remember is that you will have multiple appetites on your program and they will most certainly not all agree with one another all the time.

Providing housing that incorporates breakfast is a fantastic idea, as you will know that students are starting their day right (if they wake up in time). If possible, you might also consider utilizing a local university cafeteria. Providing a prepaid cafeteria card with a fixed amount will give students the freedom to choose when to eat and when to sleep late.

A popular semester program has offered a weekly per diem to the students since its inception. Every Monday morning, the faculty leader gives each student a sum of euros equal to their weekly per diem. Students can use the money to charge up their cafeteria card, purchase groceries, or eat out. A Monday disbursement also gives the director a way of checking in with students to make sure they have returned from weekend travel.

If your program is housed at a field station, all meals should be included unless the station is within walking distance of a local village where there are restaurants. Even so, if you do not provide dinner and students are walking at night with little or no lighting, you may be putting them in danger. For fieldwork, you should provide lunch or brief students fully on what the lunch provisions will be. If appropriate time is not provided to seek out lunch on their own, then you must clarify for students what they should do to provide for their lunch; if there are no coolers available, they should also know to bring nothing that requires refrigeration.

If your program is located in a large city, don't include all program meals as a group. And if you do, be prepared for the question from participants about getting refunds for the meals they do not wish to take. When available, part of study abroad should include the challenge (and benefit) of ordering food individually. Students need to be able to explore their language and culinary abilities, likes and dislikes. If you are ordering every meal for them, they miss out on this challenge. They may want to explore new places and foods, so trust your students to make it to a restaurant and back. Remember, their tastes and preferences are different than yours.

Above all, this is another area where transparency and coaching are extremely important. Students need to know what to expect, and be prepared, to reduce the 'what have I gotten myself into' response. If students know what to expect, they complain very little. When it comes to food, there is no such thing as too much orientation, or too much coaching and preparation, but unfortunately there is too little offered most of the time.

Activities
Activities, guest lectures, and excursions can make or break your program. Scheduling is vital, but the relevance of these activities is also crucial. Of course, you want to expose your students to the local culture, but you also have to make the program academically viable. A literature class that includes a walking tour with a licensed guide can take students into the historical sections of the city and target the literature of the course. Think about all the possibilities, and you will spend more time trying to cut things out rather than add things new:

- City tour (walking, via bus, via boat)
- Museum visit(s)
- Targeted sections of a museum
- Guest lectures
- City libraries
- Visits with authors, politicians, business owners
- Garden tours
- Castle and home tours
- Government, parliament visits
- Radio, TV, newspaper visits
- Theatrical performances
- Backstage theatre tours
- Factory tours (cars, wine, paint, furniture, you name it)

Tours can be customized to fit the unique needs of your group. An engineering class visiting a brewery should be provided with information on relevant engineering aspects of the brewery to enhance their experience and relevancy to the class. A generic tour that combines your group with another class, or tourists, may not be academically focused, but in this case, you can alert your students ahead of time and challenge them to ask academically relevant questions. Alternately, you can regroup after a tour to debrief or assign a paper that asks students to indicate how the things they saw relate to the field of study.

Start with the local tourism board. Calling the Korean Tourist Organization can score excellent visit ideas, assistance in setting up appointments abroad, literature to pass out to participants, and even free theatre tickets (normally $45 each) for a program of twenty! Also, never underestimate the power of a great guidebook and some time spent on the Internet.

2.8 Budget

Accurate budgeting is crucial to program success. Under budgeting can create problems for you and your students. Over budgeting can make your program more expensive and less attractive. If your study abroad office manages faculty-led programs, there are probably policies that pertain to the budget. If there are no policies that guide the budget, or worse, no study abroad office, then ask your administration and university counsel to develop some. In the meantime, expect to handle overages with a personal credit card or payroll deduction.

The price you advertise to students is a contract, so to speak. It cannot go over, even if you budget poorly. On the other hand, a program can be cancelled because of insufficient enrollment and funds. In this case, participants can agree to pay more for the program or they may decide it isn't worth it or they cannot afford it. When designing your program, consider the price ceiling of your students. What can students afford to spend to study abroad at your institution? Are most of your students on financial aid? This will help determine your ceiling. Consult your study abroad office for structural advice and appropriate pricing.

Consider every detail of your program expenses before advertising a price. Use whatever you need to create a budget and clarify finances, and be sure to include all of the necessary components that you would like to cover with the program fee (tuition, housing, meals, activities, travel, insurance, communication, faculty expenses, faculty stipend, administrative fees, and incidentals).

When listing your program fee in printed materials you should indicate what the fee covers, as well as what it does not cover. Students need to know how to plan for those things that are *not* included in the stated program cost.

Sample Budget Worksheet		
Program:	**Site:**	**Dates:**
Faculty Leader:	**Account No:**	
University/Administrative Costs		
Tuition		
Books		
Promotional materials		
Phone, phone card, other phone usage		
Student Application Fee		
Subtotal University/Administrative Costs		
University/Administrative Cost per student		
Instructional Costs		
Classroom space		
Equipment		
Copies		
Books, materials		
Other:		
Subtotal Instructional Costs		
Instructional Cost per student		
Program Costs		
Airport Shuttle (vehicle usage + driver) for Departure		

Airport Shuttle (vehicle usage + driver) for Return				
Airfare				
Visa Fees				
Airport transfers				
Housing	*Accommodation Name and Dates*	*Nights*	*Cost /night*	*Total*
Meals	Group Meals			
	Individual Meals Estimate Stipends			
Activities, Entrance fees, Excursions	*Activity Name*	*Date*	*Cost*	*Total*
Transportation onsite and local	*Type*	*Date*	*Cost*	*Total*
Contingency/Tips	*Expense*	*Date*	*Cost*	
Insurance (per month)				
Subtotal Program Costs per student				

Faculty Costs		
Airfare		
Visa Fees		
Housing		
Daily meals		
Activities		
Local Transportation		
Travel to/from US Airport		
Insurance (per month)		
Subtotal Faculty Leader Cost		
Faculty Leader Cost per student		
Total Student Charge:	**Participant Minimum:**	

Tuition

Tuition may be handled in many different ways. Some universities charge tuition separately to the general fund, some charge tuition to specific account, sometimes there is a tuition remission process, and sometimes tuition is built into your budget (and program fee) to cover a stipend or salary for the faculty. Check with your study abroad office to find out how to factor this in.

Housing

When pricing your housing options, be realistic. Get quotes for the exact time of year and area of the city where you are planning to execute your program. Also, call the accommodation provider. If you establish a relationship, then you may get a better rate, especially if the provider knows you will be coming back in the future to occupy another large block of rooms. Ask yourself the following questions before getting started:

- Will participants be housed in single, double, triple, or quad rooms?
- How will choosing a particular accommodation limit the program participation (space maximums, curfews, etc.)?

- Where is the housing located? Consider safety and ease of transport to the programmed activities.
- You, the faculty leader, need a private room if possible or a shared room with your co-leader. You may have to manage confidential information and be available at all hours to respond to emergencies.

Meals

When is it convenient to provide meals and when is it inconvenient to do so? This should be a major consideration when figuring the meal cost. Including breakfast at your accommodation is a great way to ensure that students at least are getting one full meal per day. But having students grab their own lunch during a busy day might be the better choice, unless you are based at a field station where there are no other existing options. Students may also wish to dine according to their own taste. Before you plan meals for the group, ask yourself the following questions:

- How much time is available daily to eat as a group? Eating as a large group always takes longer than dining individually, sometimes twice as long.
- How much variety is available in the provided meals?
- Will it be cheaper for students to eat on their own than it would be to provide every/certain meal(s)?

Activities

Any activity that will be a required component of the program should be included in the program fee. Some providers may not accept credit cards and therefore bringing cashier's checks or university checks may be necessary. Be sure to find this out well in advance because if checks must be issued from your university, there will likely be paperwork to complete for the vendor abroad. Ask yourself the following questions:

- Which activities are intricately tied to the goals of the course and are therefore required for all participants?

- Which activities can and should be cut because they are adding cost that is not tied to the goals of the course?
- If your budget is still over the desired limit, which of the required activities can you cut (if any)?
- How can you further cut costs? For example, excursions close to each other should take place on the same day.

Travel
Travel includes organized movement from program start to end. You get to decide what will be organized and what will not. It may or may not be convenient to arrange transportation to and from the international airport at home. Generally, if you've arranged group airfare, then you should also arrange for airport transfers onsite. On-site transportation will include a number of point-to-point options, by subway, taxi, city bus, coach, train, and/or ferry.

If your program does not offer a group flight, you may eliminate the airport transfer and instead have students meet you at the program site. You may also decide to include a local transit pass so that group travel is not necessary but instead participants can meet at local activities during specific times, thus eliminating the herds. Whatever the method, there should be budget considerations for getting from point to point for each *required* activity. You should not expect students to purchase individual bus tickets each time you head out for an excursion. In addition to the time wasted, students will complain about the hidden costs later.

Points to consider:

- Will you provide transport to the airport of departure?
- Can you find a group flight as inexpensively as an individual flights on the Internet?
- Will you require a group flight? Will you book it? How will it be paid for: by your university, by students directly to the provider, by students to you?

- If you have a group flight, will students have the option to book their own flight as well?
- What is the least expensive yet most efficient use of on-site transportation for daily activities and excursions?

Insurance
Health insurance should be mandatory, and therefore built into your program fee. Check with your study abroad office for details. The study abroad office and subsequently, your university, may have a contract with a specific international insurance provider for a specific plan. If your university does not require insurance for study abroad programs, then it is your responsibility to ensure that your students purchase individual plans. If a student gets ill or worse, you will need provisions and assistance.

Your basic insurance should include medical and accident coverage, medical evacuation, and repatriation of remains. You should also consider any affordable coverage for quarantine, pregnancy, mental health issues, alcohol-related accidents, bedside reunion (the cost to fly a loved one to the site in case of participant hospitalization), political and security evacuation, and natural disaster evacuation. Whatever you end up paying will be minimal relative to the cost that you, your student, or your university will pay in the event of a disaster without insurance.

> The director of an England program discovered on-site that she was having a miscarriage. She spent several days and nights in the hospital, received emergency surgery, and eventually also a blood transfusion. Her husband flew over to be by her side midway through the week. The costs incurred to her were covered first by her domestic insurance at the regular policy rate of 80% while her study abroad insurance then covered the other 20%.

It's always better when everyone on the program carries the same insurance. If you experience a security situation and need to be evacuated, yet only four of your participants carry security evacuation, you will be left deciding what to do with the rest of the group. You cannot manage a full-scale group emergency for 25 participants with 25 different insurance providers. Any responsible insurance provider will also take care of logistics for needed evacuations and medical payments. As a faculty leader, you will be communicating with students and parents.

Some insurance companies may use lack of official registration with the US Department of State as an excuse *not* to cover claims from abroad. Thus, be sure that all of your participants register their travel plans with the US Department of State.

Insurance for International Travel

Health-related Necessities:
1. Basic medical and accident coverage
2. Bedside reunion
3. Medical evacuation
4. Repatriation of remains

Internationally Relevant Add-ons:
1. Quarantine coverage
2. Coverage for pre-existing pregnancy
3. Coverage for alcohol-related accidents

4. Loss of luggage
5. Trip interruption
6. Political/Security evacuation
7. Natural disaster evacuation

Points to consider:

- Does your university have a health insurance provider for international travel? If so, what is the cost? How do you sign up for it? How do students sign up for it?

- If your university does not have a health insurance provider, can you endorse one for your program? Is there a bid process for this at the university level?
- What is the coverage needed for your participants?

Communication

You may need to communicate back home with the study abroad office or other university officials, particularly in the event of an emergency. You may also need to communicate with students who are out on their own. Consider all the options and compare costs for purchasing or renting an overseas cell phone, using your own cellular phone abroad, satellite phone, email at the hotel or internet cafes, text messaging, Skype.com, or international phone cards. One location will enable the use of several options while another only one option due to its remote location. Try to plan for several avenues of communication in case one fails.

Points to consider:

- What is the relative cost of each available method of communication?
- How practical and easy is it to secure and use each available method of communication?
- If taking your own personal cell phone, how will you be reimbursed for work-related calls?

Faculty Expenses

Leader expenses should be included in the published student budget under 'tuition' or 'instructional costs' for student financial aid purposes. Include all transportation and living costs on-site, as well as your compensation according to university procedures. Faculty compensation for study abroad courses can vary dramatically from one university to another. If you are receiving release time for the study abroad course, then you will probably not receive a stipend, and vice versa. Your program expenses will be covered, but ethically, you should not attempt to collect two forms of compensation without special permission to do so.

Sometimes a faculty leader will bring along an assistant, to learn about the program, perhaps to lead it the next year, or use the experience to create a new program. There is usually no compensation for students, but sometimes a department is willing to cover all or a portion of the assistant's program expenses to keep the fee within a reasonable range. If you're not so fortunate, then you may need to figure the extra cost into your program budget: flight, housing, meals, on-site transport, insurance, and activities.

Points to consider:

- Your stipend or salary comes from students. If your university allows up to $200 per student for the stipend, but your total program cost is $100 more than you anticipated, then ask yourself if you can you live with $100 per student.
- Keep your expenses to a minimum. Though you should have a private room, you do not need a suite. The same goes for meals; you need to eat, but you do not need to have five-course meals. Set a reasonable daily per diem for yourself and stick to it.

Administrative Fees
Does your university charge each student who studies abroad an administrative fee that is separate from tuition? It may be referred to as an application fee, a study abroad fee, a course fee, or an orientation fee and range from $50 and up. This fee may be required to fund the study abroad office, scholarships, or university operations. If administrative fees are collected, how do they help your program (webpage, marketing materials, orientation, etc.)? Depending on how they are used, some administrative fees may be figured into the budget category of tuition for the purposes of student financial aid.

Incidentals

Incidental expenses include all items not considered herein. Some of these expenses will be essential while others are superfluous. How will incidentals be covered? Will you be given a cash advance from your institution and asked to account for incidentals later or will you be expected to utilize personal funds and ask the university for reimbursement? Incidentals may include:

- Emergency expenses (taxi, medicine purchases, etc.)
- Orientation costs for food, space, and materials
- Marketing materials such as fliers, brochures, posters, CD's, DVD's, t-shirts, or food to offer during an informational session
- Host family gifts or closing program party
- Tips for guides, drivers, and hotel concierge
- Program giveaways (water bottles, luggage tags, etc.).

2.9 The Last Word

How do you create a study abroad program at your university? This chapter has detailed the many points you should consider while building a program from the ground up. We know that such a complex topic is intimidating and that you may or may not have the support of a study abroad office. Either way we hope that the tools provided here will help you get started.

Building a study abroad program involves much work with much reward. Fortunately, you have the ability to determine how best to organize and implement your efforts. Whether you choose to do it yourself, contract with a third-party, or go with some combination of a multitude of other options, you can negotiate and make good decisions. Working through budget issues and questions with your university will help you determine how to move forward. All of these components go hand-in-hand with making the best possible program and experience for your students, your institution, and yes, you, too.

Chapter Three: Faculty Responsibilities

If you have a study abroad office, or another campus reference point for study abroad, check to see if there are any guidelines for faculty-led programs. If there is no study abroad office, then be sure to read Chapter 6 for the university perspective, especially if you are asked to establish a structure. By nature of your position and program, you may become the most knowledgeable person on campus and begin guiding others through the program development process.

It's easy to feel lost and overwhelmed without the assistance of a highly knowledgeable study abroad office. Don't be anxious, this chapter will help. As you progress through, create a set of questions for your university administration or legal counsel. Meet with them to determine expectations of the university. This does two things: first, it ensures you have the support of the university throughout the process, and second, it creates a set of guidelines that can be used for other faculty and future programs abroad.

3.1 Responsible Study Abroad Faculty Orientation

If your university offers a faculty orientation for study abroad programs, be sure to take part. It may be required and should provide you with expectations for faculty-led programs, as well as the university's stance on your responsibilities. Content usually covers risk management for the university, liability, and what is expected of you in terms of academics, fiscal management, crisis management, disciplinary management, and program logistics. Even if not required, attendance at such an orientation shows due diligence on your behalf.

What is your authority before, during, and after the program? Do you have the ability to cancel programs, discipline students, or mandate orientations? Will you be required to take an Assistant Director, a second faculty or staff chaperone who will assist you with program logistics? What are the procedures in case of a crisis? Are crisis protocols in place? Is there financial backing for emergencies? Are there personal financial implications for you if your program goes over budget? You need to know the policies so that you can cover yourself from the beginning of the process to the end of the program.

You also need to know what is handled by the study abroad office and what is handled by you. Who signs service contracts? Who puts together a web page and fliers for the program? Are applications turned in to the study abroad office or to you? Who makes admissions decisions? Do you develop a student orientation on your own or do you share this process with study abroad staff? How do students seek financial aid or schedule for the study abroad class? If there is a set of existing procedures, you need to be aware of them so you can properly advise students.

3.2 Pre-Departure and On-Site Orientation

It is our legal duty in higher education to assure that all students participate in a relevant and appropriate pre-departure orientation, *before* they study abroad. Your study abroad office likely organizes a general pre-departure orientation for all students, which you can pair with a program-specific session. If you do not have a study abroad office, or your study abroad office doesn't organize any pre-departure orientations, refer to Chapter 6 for other important items to include in your agenda.

Because you need to know what students are told, and subsequently what they should know, it is highly recommended that you attend any student orientations offered by the study abroad office. Have students been warned about alcohol consumption? What are the university rules and regulations regarding conduct on the program abroad? How have students been prepared for emergency or crisis situations? Attending the orientations will provide you with the background and support to properly manage your students and program internationally.

In addition to general health and safety information, students need to know what to pack for your program, cultural do's and don'ts, and much more. Set orientation dates well in advance, and inform students early on. Also, set clear parameters for those who miss. If you have a large group of students with scheduling issues, consider videotaping each orientation. Videotaping ensures that anyone who makes up the session receives the same information, and if you have guest students participating, you can post the video online, or mail a copy, for them to review along with a verification test. You can also work with your technology office to conduct a live, interactive session through videoconference, Skype.com, or another medium.

Pre-Departure Orientation
(Sample Agenda)

General Information (for all programs and students)
A. Packing
B. Electrical Issues
C. Departing the US
D. While Abroad
E. Taking Money
F. Health and Safety
G. Crisis Management: Problem vs. Emergency
H. Conduct/Behavior
I. Cultural Immersion

Break-Out Session (specifically for your program)
A. Travel Details
    1) Distribution of airline tickets and itinerary details
    2) Will the group be transported to the airport together for departure from the US? Will someone be at the airport to pick them up or do they need to take a taxi? If students will go directly into a city tour, this information will help them pack and dress appropriately

---

so their cameras are readily available and they aren't in sweatpants when they arrive.

    3) Luggage restrictions, extra costs

    4) Any specific instructions about meeting at the airport at home or abroad, or getting to the program site

    5) Will students have time for independent travel and exploration? If so, are there any sign-out rules for the evening, weekend, or week?

B. Logistical Details

    1) Weather information

    2) Specific dress code (if applicable)

    3) Will students need any special equipment?

    4) Where is the accommodation? What is the contact information? Does the accommodation provide towels and washcloths?

    5) Which meals are provided, if any?

    6) Currency conversion and money usage

        i. How much money should students have for the program?

        ii. Are ATM machines easily accessible? Are they safe to use?

        iii. Are debit and credit cards accepted widely?

        iv. What is the local currency and the exchange rate? Is it likely to change while you're abroad?

    7) Program itinerary

        i. For short-term programs, daily schedule

        ii. For long-term programs, more details regarding scheduled group excursions, activities, and course timetable

    8) How can students communicate back home? Are US cell phones advisable? Are internet cafes widely available?

C. Course Details

    1) Syllabus distribution

    2) Do students register themselves for the course or will you register for them?

     3) Will the course be assigned a letter grade, pass/fail, or credit/no credit?

     4) Will grades be submitted on the regular university schedule?

D. Safety and Health

     1) Are there specific areas of the city they should avoid?

     2) Are there program tips to offer regarding navigation or areas of the city where pickpockets are rampant?

     3) What do students do when they are feeling ill? Who is the first point of contact for illness?

     4) Is insurance provided? What does insurance cover?

E. Conduct/Behavior

     1) What is the general conduct you expect of students abroad?

     2) What are the boundaries? Is there a 'three strikes and you're out' rule?

     3) Are there specific conduct expectations based on the type of housing or for certain excursions?

F. Emergency Response

     1) What constitutes an emergency?

     2) Whom do students contact first in an emergency? Do they have emergency cards with program contact details? Will students be provided with local cell phone numbers and/or leader room numbers on site?

     3) What is the meeting point in case of a national emergency that takes communication systems down? What is expected of students in this situation?

G. Cultural Details

     1) Major cultural differences or practices in the host country, region, and/or city

     2) Tipping

     3) Food differences

     4) Language lesson

Student Panel, Questions, Concerns

It is also wise to build an on-site orientation into the program schedule within the first 24 hours of arrival. On-site orientation should serve as a reminder about important issues, but should not repeat all of the information covered in pre-departure. Some specifics will need to be reviewed for those who have forgotten, but once you're on-site, there is also new information that you can provide to students that was not available before.

In the first 24 hours, students should be taught how to use local transportation, shown the meeting point for tour departure and crisis response, and reminded of all the cultural do's and don'ts. Getting to know the physical aspects of a site, and how to get from one point to another, are very important for student safety and well-being. A well-planned on-site orientation that begins and ends from student housing may go a long way in ensuring students do not develop a bunker mentality and have undue fears of their surroundings. Reminders about a buddy system, areas to avoid, or curfew requirements are also necessary.

Faculty leaders often pay more attention to student physical well-being than emotional well-being. Think about the current students that you serve. A call to the Counseling Center on your campus can provide you with an accurate view of mental health within your student body. If 60% of your student body is on medication or seeking some sort of counseling for mental health, you can assume the same percentage for your program. Students may or may not disclose this information to you; therefore, it is important that you do everything possible to prevent unnecessary mental and emotional strain and talk about culture shock openly.

As long as mental health conditions are managed, there is no reason for worry or concern. Students with mental health concerns are encouraged to discuss study abroad and its challenges with their counselor or physician. Those who do are more likely to succeed on a study abroad program than those who don't. Take the extra time to ensure that all emotional as well as physical concerns are considered in the program's structure. The extra time spent in an initial on-site orientation to make sure each student understands program expectations, how to get around, and which areas to avoid, goes a long way to decrease anxiety for everyone in the group.

On-Site Orientation Agenda

A. Behavior expectations
B. Academic expectations
C. Housing reminders
D. Travel information:
    1) Hand out tickets for entrances and final itineraries (strongly suggest that you have them sign for these)
    2) City tour
    3) How to use local transportation
    4) Cultural information: tipping, queuing, non-verbal cues, personal space, etc.
E. Local safety reminders
    1) Common areas for pick-pockets
    2) Avoiding certain areas
    3) Buddy system
    4) Remind students we cannot get them out of jail
F. Emergency information
    1) Contacts—emergency cards
    2) Meeting point for emergencies
    3) Hotel business card

3.3 Know Study Abroad Processes and Procedures

It's important to understand your institution's paperwork and procedures for study abroad programs, so that you can guide students through the process. It's difficult to recruit students without knowing how to help them fill out application materials, answer their questions about financial aid and scholarships, etc. If your study abroad office doesn't provide you with this information, then seek it out. Students will assume you are the expert on everything related to your program, and if they see that you are not, they may decide not to go abroad or choose another program instead of yours.

If your institution has a study abroad office, the paperwork and processes will likely be standardized and channeled through the office. Learn about the steps and what is involved, as well as how you will be included in the application and selection process. If you are creating the application process yourself, consider the following components: application, transcript, reference letter, and essay, as well as other paperwork. Consider your minimum requirements, but also how you will admit students (first-come first-serve, points on a rubric, etc.), and how you will wait-list and reject candidates, if you have more applications than you do space in your program.

The application and follow-up process for any study abroad program should consider the following:

- **Statement of Responsibility** – This is your program's legal form. It will usually address behavior expectations, administrative logistics, any health and safety standards, academic credit, travel arrangements, program changes, financial obligations, early departure, and various policies, as well as waivers and indemnification clauses for you and your university. Work with your General Counsel to compose this important document that your students will sign.

- **Applications Abroad** – If you are utilizing a third-party provider or a host institution abroad, then they will need information about your participants. They may require a list of names, or additional forms or information such as housing or roommate preferences, as well as individual needs (i.e. allergic to dogs or vegetarian, if staying with a host family). Check with your partners before the application process begins.

- **Medical Information Form** – It is imperative to have a university-approved process that considers medical information, not for admissions purposes (as this is illegal), but to help accommodate your students in their program abroad, whether they have a medical problem, an allergy, or a mental health issue. Work with your health center and General Counsel to come up with the right process that will help you and your students without violating laws.

- **Disciplinary History** – Are students allowed to study abroad on your campus if they are under review for a disciplinary sanction or they are on academic probation? It is generally not a good idea to admit students who've had significant behavior problems on campus, or who have exhibited harm to self or others. Find out what your university criterion are and build a disciplinary check into your paperwork process.

- **Judicial History** – Students may have a criminal history without having a disciplinary record on campus. Excluding minor traffic violations, have they been arrested, charged, or convicted of a felony or misdemeanor?

- **Flight Itinerary** – If students are permitted or even required to book their own flights, then you will need a copy of their flight itineraries. If something goes wrong, you'll be glad you took this very important step.

- **Passport Signature Page** – It is easier to replace a lost or stolen passport when you have a copy of the signature page. Don't rely on students to bring their own copy; instead, have them provide you with one before departure.

- **Insurance** – Is insurance provided by your university or through the study abroad office? Is the cost figured into the program budget? How do students (and you) enroll? Where do they get their cards? What is covered (and not covered)?

Financial Aid and Scholarship Process

Federal financial aid applies to the cost of study abroad programs. Your campus may already be accustomed to dealing with study abroad program budgets and have a standard process in place to apply federal aid to study abroad programs. In this case, your study abroad office will help you with the procedures required for your students. However, it is also possible that your financial aid office has not dealt with this before. As such, you may find yourself working directly with the personnel in this office to determine what is required of students and how you can work together to make funding decisions in the student's favor. Prepare a program budget to start this process.

Are there general study abroad scholarships on your campus? If so, what are the deadlines? Are there study abroad scholarships or grants for students in your academic college? You should know what, if any, university funding exists for students in your program and encourage them to apply. If you are leading a semester program, you should also inquire about the usage of university merit scholarships, grants, and other forms of financial aid that are typically allocated during the semester and academic year.

3.4 Recruitment

Your ability to recruit students for your program will ultimately determine if it is successful or not. Find your niche early so that you can build a solid base. Most faculty report that recruiting for their program was harder than they expected it to be. Rare is the program that has too many students apply without a great deal of marketing on behalf of the faculty. Be prepared to employ multiple tools to draw students and see your program to fruition. One information session or speaking to two or three classes will not make it happen. You must be continually recruiting every qualified student you meet.

When you speak to a class or club, collect the names and email addresses of students who express interest. Also, keep the names and email addresses of those who contact you for more information. Send follow-up messages every so often, reminding students that the program deadline is approaching, or highlighting a play, event, or performance that is part of your program destination. Current events in the international location can and should also be shared. These tidbits remind students about the program and help to maintain their interest.

There are three common platforms from which you can recruit students: a campus, a consortium, or a nation. Consider your ideal participant and target your efforts around the program's entry requirements. If your program is for students with two years of coursework in a particular field, then you have a narrow and limited audience that is easily identifiable. If your program requires students to speak a foreign language, then again, your target population is clear. On the other hand, if your program offers a basic-level course that could be used as an elective for all science students, you have a wide audience and many possibilities for recruitment.

If your program is offered via a consortium or open to students across the nation, then further interesting challenges await your recruiting efforts. On your campus, you have a captive audience and have built relationships with students and faculty who trust you. However, students who stumble upon your course through consortium materials or online directories do not have the benefit of being enthralled by your knowledge and charm. You will have to work harder to create a niche for your program, to promote it effectively with these audiences. One website, AbroadScout.com is known for faculty-led programs and search-friendly features.

Campus-Wide Recruitment
Your study abroad office should have tips about how to recruit effectively on campus and will likely help. Look at this office as a wholesaler of programs. They may be able to help you with fliers, web design, posting information, scheduling presentations, study

abroad fairs and other events. They can also help with program logistics like application materials, financial aid, and course credit. Whatever they do, it will be the same for all study abroad programs offered by your university. Giving special preference or treatment to any one program would go against their purpose, which is to manage education abroad and help each student find the best fit for his/her personal, academic, and career goals.

You are the retailer of your program, and you are what it will take to sell the program amid the competition. Do not rely on your study abroad office to sell your program, but rather to support *you* in the process. It is important to come up with a recruitment plan that maximizes contact with your target audience. Focus on classes, clubs, and other student groups that match your target audience. For example, if you are teaching an outdoor recreation course abroad with no prerequisites, then your target audience is recreation and physical education majors, and students in other health sciences, too. You could target every class in your department, students in education, the fitness center, and student clubs that center on recreation activities.

Remember, your program may be competing with those of third-party providers or even your faculty colleagues. Students on your campus are usually not required to study only with home faculty but can choose from hundreds of options offered nationwide.

A myriad of other activities for campus-wide recruitment include: holding information sessions, hanging fliers and posters strategically around campus, attending campus study abroad fairs, and advertising your program through the university calendar, intranet, university website, radio station, television station, and newspaper. Every institution is different and the allowances for using any one of these marketing ideas may vary. For example, you may not be permitted to post your program on the campus intranet, but perhaps you will be allowed access to an email list for all students in your department. Find the parameters on your campus for advertising and maximize them. Do everything you can imagine could be done to reach your target audience.

Facebook, Twitter, and other social media are also being used to market study abroad programs. If you are not proficient in these forms of outreach, any number of your students would probably be happy to give you a tutorial in exchange for some extra credit, or manage advertising for you in exchange for perhaps a reduced program fee.

Facebook allows you to create Pages and Groups for your program. Interested students and other faculty who 'like' your Page or 'join' your Group will increase its visibility. Also, pages can have open permissions so that anyone can follow. When your program is abroad, you can post photos so that moms and dads, university officials, and prospective university students can see what's going on. It becomes a great way to catalogue the program, keep in touch with everyone back at home, advertise how study abroad is valued on your campus, and introduce the pals of your students to study abroad (the ultimate recruiting tool).

Twitter is a completely different animal. You create an account and post information about anything you want at any time from anywhere. The trick with Twitter is that you must have followers. The more followers, the more people will see your information. Twitter is not used to browse profiles, so unless you already have a following, it will probably not be as useful for advertising your program. You can build up a following through contests, however. Talk to your students to find out how they decide whom to 'follow' on Twitter.

Facebook and Twitter both sell advertising space. You can buy advertisements that target members of a network. This type of advertising has proven to be very effective; however, you may have to pay out-of-pocket if your study abroad office does not have advertising funds to support faculty-led programs. To solve this problem, consider building funds for advertising into your program budget.

Consider the following recruiting tips for faculty:

- Inform your departmental colleagues of the course you are teaching abroad.
- Ask your colleagues if you can speak to their classes for as little as three minutes to pass out fliers or as long as 30 minutes to show slides and talk about program details.
- Hold information sessions with food and invite study abroad personnel to these sessions to help with the application and financial questions as needed.
- Visit the residence halls to hold information sessions. Bring along past study abroad participants or international students, and perhaps organize a Q&A panel.
- Staff a table at the Study Abroad Fair.
- Post announcements on the university intranet, newsletter, and calendar of events.
- Hang up fliers or posters across campus, but especially in those buildings where students are attending classes that seem to be a natural fit for your program.
- Create T-shirts with program information.
- Put your program details up on the study abroad website.
- Create a Facebook page or group and invite your students to become a fan or join it.
- Tweet (Twitter) about your program as it is being planned and later while it is going on. It is never too early to start recruiting for the next round.
- Talk to the students in your own classes as much as possible.
- Keep a list of students who have expressed interest and send emails to them every couple of weeks about what you have recently learned about the country, events that will be happening there while the program is going on, scholarship announcements, deadlines, etc.
- Fill in the program name, course, and term on each applica-

tion you give to students and anything else to make it easier for them to complete it.

Consortium-Wide Recruitment

Offering your course through a member-based consortium allows students from member institutions to participate in your course alongside students from your own campus. This makes recruiting a bit easier with a wider pool from which you can draw students. However, it makes marketing more complex with greater competition among a larger number of programs.

The cost of program brochures, booklets, website upkeep, and other advertising done by a consortium is usually shared among members or managed by a head office. What you need to think about is how your program, displayed in a four-page spread of other programs in London, is going to stand out. It may be that your program's price, dates, and location are the same as or similar to the other programs. So, what will make students pick your program over the rest? What makes it more interesting and relevant? The title should be catchy, and the description should explain what you're going to do in London, tying together academics and location in a crystal-clear way.

Try to establish contact with other study abroad offices within the consortium, so they understand your program details, course, itinerary, etc. Ultimately, it will be their choice to allow you to recruit on their campus (or not).

Answering emails from students who belong to member institutions can be tricky. They may ask for more details about what you will be doing in your course or program, but they may also ask how the course will transfer into their institution or their degree program, how their financial aid applies to the program, if tuition payments must be made to their home institution, and more. All of these questions are institution-specific and must be answered by the home university. In every case, make sure you send the student back to their study abroad office or consortium campus representative to seek out the correct information.

National Recruitment

Across the nation, you will be competing for students who have thousands of other faculty-led or third-party provider program options available to them. For this reason, national recruiting is better suited to unique, niche programs that fit a particular genre of student or field of study. If you are doing the grand tour of Europe, then don't expect to pull students from too many other colleges and universities; there is one of these at nearly every institution that does study abroad. However, if your program is unique (Archaeological Dig in Belgium, Viking Studies in Scandinavia) and there aren't too many other programs just like yours, then your best strategy could be to target the market across the nation. Also, if you have built up a following for your research or other expertise, it will be easier for you to recruit nationwide.

To target-market your program across the nation, consider your professional listservs, organizational meetings, and online directories. AbroadScout is a study abroad portal and directory known for its high percentage of faculty-led programs. Users can search by key words, key phrases, or with the advanced program finder to find what they want and need. AbroadScout also hosts a blog and collects and averages student reviews for every program in its directory. This allows you to build up a star rating for your program that further sets it apart from the competition. Universities can create their own "customized" searchable directories, too. For more information, visit www.abroadscout.com.

If you advertise your program online, be sure to include accurate, relevant keywords on your website and in your program description. Make sure the right keyword searches turn up your program, so that students will be more likely to find it.

3.5 Finances

Fiscal management can vary wildly from one university to the next. Every campus has its own set of rules and every state its own set of regulations. Find out well in advance how to handle the finances for your study abroad program. First, find out if the study abroad or continuing education office will be acting as your agent and go-between with the university accounting office or if you will be sending paperwork directly to the accounting office. Second, find out how the university will bill students and how students can pay for the program. There are a number of options for payment depending on your university policies:

- You can bill each student's university account. This means that students pay for the program through the university, and the university then pays for outsourced services.
- Payment to you means that you are personally responsible for the fiscal execution of the program and must keep an extremely careful and accurate accounting of what you are sending out and taking in, as well as to and from whom.
- Payment can also be made directly from the students to a third-party provider or host institution that is taking care of all arrangements. Your university may charge a fee for administration and/or insurance, but no program fees.

And of course, there is always the possibility of a hybrid of two. For example, if you are using a third-party provider then students may be billed by the third-party provider but your university may also insist on charging a tuition fee or you may wish to arrange group airfare separately. In such a case, who is responsible for making sure the university accounts have been billed correct? If the study abroad office is hands-off in terms of faculty-led fiscal planning, then the answer to that question is you. If this is the case, then you will need to think about the following:

- How will program deposits be made to vendors?
- How will group airline tickets be purchased?

- If students are billed through their university accounts or by a third party directly, how will you pay for incidentals while you are on-site? What is the paperwork process for getting a cash advance and turning in the remainder?
- Will the study abroad office help with making payments?
- Will you have a university credit card for your program account? Or, will there be a university program account?

Your university will have a process for making payments. This will likely include some form of documentation required from the vendor. Find out if your university will allow wire transfers or direct deposits, or will only cut checks, and if there are certain days that checks are cut or deposits are made. What role will the study abroad office play in this process? For example, if payments are made to university accounts, does the study abroad office turn in billing for your program to the Bursar's Office? Do you?

Find out what your accounting policies are on all transactions abroad and your fiscal responsibility. Where is there leeway and where is there no flexibility? If you show up for a tour and find that payment has not been made to the provider, can you expect to be reimbursed by your university if you pay out-of-pocket? If you are issued a university credit card, when can you use it for program expenses and when can you not? Know the parameters for handling payments while on-site. Faculty leaders often encounter challenges when considering tips and other payments that do not provide receipts.

Finally, what if your program goes into the red? Who is responsible? Will your department have to cover the cost? Will this come out of your personal program stipend? Does it depend on the situation? For example, if it were an emergency that put you into the red, would it be reimbursed or forgiven by the university? Find out what the parameters are so you know where you stand in the event that you go over budget.

Finances are a huge piece of program management. If you are utilizing a third party or if your study abroad office is handling the lion's share of this for you, thank your lucky stars. Otherwise, you must find a way to manage the budget responsibly and follow the guidelines of your university to ensure that you stay within your means and reconcile the program account. Being proactive and seeking out this information ahead of time will save you a big headache in the end.

3.6 Logistical Issues
You have made the plans, reservations, and payments for your logistical arrangements. You have recruited students for a quality program. What happens if you arrive and realize the things you had planned are not available, or the quality that you were expecting is not there, or worse, is not safe? Can you make changes on-site? Can you cancel an activity? Of course you can, but how will this affect student perception, attitude, and finances? Expect the unexpected. Good planning will allow for flexibility on site.

First, it's important to have a written, signed agreement between your university and all your vendors. This agreement outlines and clarifies the services to provide, provisions to those services, and expectations, as well as indemnification. This goes a long way to alleviate contractual and cultural misunderstandings. Second, it's extremely helpful to have a back-up plan and the ability to implement it if necessary. When accessibility or safety is in question, you shouldn't hesitate for an instant, even to the financial detriment of the program.

You should have done your due diligence to investigate the site beforehand using multiple resources for safety and access approvals. However, if upon arrival you discover the housing is in an unsafe location, does not accommodate your wheelchair-bound student, or is structurally unsound, you must relocate. Consider first and foremost your responsibility for the mobility, health, safety, and well-being of program participants and staff. All reasonable and prudent measures should be taken to limit the

University's legal liabilities, while at the same time conforming to the standards of ethical practice for study abroad.

If you are not savvy with the local transportation, arrive earlier than the students and give yourself some time to learn how to navigate the city. You can also scout routes just a day or so in advance of an activity and make changes to transportation plans as you see fit. You may discover in your exploration that certain routes are under construction or close early. Be sure to check the Country Specific Information Sheet for particulars such as dangerous routes, unsafe areas, and more at Travel.State.Gov.

You are the one on the ground. The university has entrusted the students and program to you, and sometimes it will be necessary to make decisions on the spot, with no time to consult the study abroad office, or worse, you may have no study abroad office to consult. You need to have reassurance that your decisions will be supported.

> A group of US students in London had a guide who made it very clear that she did not like Americans. The guide remarked on the lack of knowledge of the students and their "egotistical American mindset." The director of the program could have requested a new guide, but did not realize it was within his power to do so. As such, the group suffered through the guide's comments for the duration of the program.

Points to consider:

- Are you comfortable making on-site logistical, and possibly last minute decisions?
- What if an important decision means the program will run into deficit? How will that be handled?
- What level of support do you have from the university?
- How often and how late does public transport run?
- Which taxis are official and safe to use? Which are not?

3.7 Health and Safety

The health and safety of all program participants is of utmost importance, which is why you see it all throughout this book. This is often one of the biggest worries of new directors. What if students get sick? How will I get help? Can I trust local doctors? Are there English-speaking doctors? What if a major national crisis occurs on-site? What are the procedures for dealing with this? Does my university have a support system and proper procedures in place to handle all types of emergencies? This section will delve into your responsibilities and questions to ask.

Building Relationships

Relationships are critical to safety and success. Taking time to develop relationships at home and abroad will pay off in the end. If you never have a safety issue, then sure enough, your relationships have played a part. If you have a crisis that requires multiple hands on deck, and you have all the hands you need, then your relationships have worked in your favor. Relationships can run from personal or professional ties to contracted services for payment.

Though never 100% guaranteed, student safety is best managed by the development of close interpersonal relationships between the faculty, students, and host-country community. On both long and short-term programs, this occurs when students are seen as extended family members in the community and not just visitors. Relationships help pave the way for many educational and social opportunities otherwise not available. They also become the basis for new emotional and even academic support systems within the country. Building the support of local authorities will go far in seeking the help you need, when you need it.

Relationship building at home is vital to program safety as well. Who will be the point of contact in case of an emergency? Who contacts families or the media if needed? What financial resources are at your disposal during emergencies? You will need to develop relationships with key individuals on campus in order to ensure sufficient support while you're abroad.

When building a new program in Costa Rica with a partner on-site, the director had little knowledge of the location. Thus, risky activities such as white-water rafting and zip-lining required further investigation of local safety standards. The partner was more than happy to track down details even though other US universities had never asked for these assurances before.

Points to consider:

- In your program planning, who have you included from the home campus?
- From an international location, who can you call 24/7?
- How extensive are your contacts on-site? Can you reach them at any time?

Basic Safety Measures
As faculty leaders or study abroad office staff, we have a duty to inform our students. Transparency in program safety planning is highly recommended. We increase our liability when we fail to inform students of all that we know or all that we should have known. What areas are unsafe? What has the US Department of State recommended we do to stay safe? What vaccinations have been recommended by the Center for Disease Control? To lessen liability and keep students well, we must properly inform them in advance.

The Peace Corps takes an integrated approach to preparation. Through language, cross-cultural, and health and safety instruction, preparation is designed to raise the Volunteer's awareness of their new environment, build their capacity to muddle through the many challenges they will face, and provide the tools they will need to adopt a safe and appropriate lifestyle. Students should receive similar preparation, and understand policies and procedures as well as their responsibility to abide by them.

But safety is more than preparing students. We have to choose the right sites, monitor local unrest and other possible challenges, and maintain responsiveness to student safety and health needs on-site. Safety auditing begins the minute we choose a site and ends when everyone is home again at the end of the program. Your groundwork thus plays a crucial role in preparing students for safe program participation. For this reason, it is always helpful to visit the international site before you plan a program. If funds are not available for site visits, consider creating your program, at least the first time, in cooperation with a third-party provider that is already working in the city or country.

Once on-site, familiarize your students with the location through city tours, scavenger hunts, and mapping exercises. This will help them feel comfortable and increase their ability to get around on their own. The initial on-site orientation is an excellent learning tool that can set the stage for health and safety throughout the program. Seek to raise awareness of the new environment, show the safest walking routes to important places, and show students how to pick up social cues, respond to unwanted attention, and develop personal coping and safety strategies.

There is never an exhaustive list of activities or plans for ensuring a student's health and safety abroad but here are a few tried and proven methods:

- **Institute a buddy system** and when you are on tours you will never forget anyone. Consider pairing students who do not know each other well and are not rooming together to augment your group dynamics. Students who are good friends are too often 'lost' together.

- **Consider a curfew** – Curfews are not fun, but if you have a younger crowd or if your housing requires students to be back by a certain hour, it could be a blessing in disguise. If you don't want to institute a curfew but wish to have knowledge of student entry and exit, consider having them sign-in and -out at the front desk or on your room door. Make sure students are told of the curfew in their pre-departure orientation so they can work out any complaining or problems with the curfew at home and not on site.

- **Carry a local cell phone** – Providing students with a local number to call can do much for relieving student and parent stress. Knowing they can reach you anytime of the day or night makes students feel safe even if they never need to use it. If you have a co-leader, share the duty.

- **Scout routes ahead of time** – Carve out time to scout your routes to activities and events in advance. This can avoid undue stress and eliminate possible challenges when you're with a big group of students.

- **Set clear conduct rules** – Alcohol-related incidents are the most common form of misconduct. Set clear parameters for students concerning alcohol consumption on your program. Also, be very clear about drugs.

Set parameters for yourself and any accompanying faculty or staff. Alcohol consumption with students puts you into murky waters that could end in a legal battle.

Points to consider:

- Have you been transparent with students by providing CDC recommendations, consular information sheets, and other safety knowledge you have of the location?

- How will you familiarize students with the site prior to departure? And once they are there?
- Will you institute a nightly curfew or have a sign-in and – out process to keep track of students?
- Where are your primary and secondary meeting locations in case of a local emergency?
- Are you prepared to support your decisions in court? Have you exercised due diligence?

Common Health and Safety Issues

There are many health and safety challenges that can arise when taking groups of students abroad. These are not all site-related. Your students and co-leaders board the plane with a medical history already packed. Directing a program abroad becomes a balancing act in managing on-site health and safety with the level of disclosure that your participants provide. Common health and safety issues on programs abroad include:

- **Finding medications abroad** – Though we instruct students to physically count the number of pills in their prescription bottle before taking off, they sometimes don't listen, or they decide to stop taking prescriptions prior to departure because they 'feel fine.' Furthermore, any participant can get sick at any time and need medication while abroad.

- **Undisclosed illnesses** – Use of psychotropic medication among today's students is more common than ever before, and mental health issues are frequently left off medical forms for a variety of reasons. During the application process, remind students that their information will be kept confidential and their truthfulness will only be used to accommodate their program experience.

- **Alcohol-related accidents** – In many countries abroad, students have reached the legal drinking age, and many students unfortunately take their new freedom too far. You can help curtail this by keeping them busy during high drinking times or simply educating them about alcohol in other countries and how culturally unacceptable it is to get drunk and become the stereotypically loud and obnoxious.

- **Stranger danger** –We learn this in elementary school but by the time our students are abroad, they have thrown the important principle of 'stranger danger' out the window. They tell strangers where they are housed, invite them to their hotel rooms, and go on dates after a 5-minute encounter in the subway. Caution students that their defenses may be lower due to the euphoria of the international experience and they should therefore scrupulously avoid poor judgment.

- **Sexual activity** – Students arrive abroad and immediately enter what they deem a fantasyland, forgetting even the most basic safety measures they would institute for themselves at home. This can result in a higher level of sexual activity and could finish with bringing home an unwanted souvenir. The perception that no one back home will know tends to make students more open to behaviors they would otherwise avoid.

Points to consider:

- What housing rules will you set to help eliminate compromising situations for students who may forget the stranger-danger principle?
- Where are the nearest doctors, pharmacies, and hospitals? What are the hours of operation and entry procedures for emergency and non-emergency treatment?
- Are common medications available over-the-counter? Or will students need to seek medical attention and obtain prescriptions for what would be considered OTC at home?

Medical Disclosures are Voluntary

Your students should be required to submit medical information. However, medical disclosure is always at the participant's own discretion unless your university will allow you the requirement of a physician-approved form. Even if you do receive a medical form signed by a physician, a participant could seek approval to travel from a physician who has not diagnosed him before and so has no knowledge of the student's medical history.

Hopefully you or your study abroad office can help persuade students to disclose medical information for their own benefit. Remind students that this information is important should they need help on-site. Explain that the information will not be shared carelessly and will not jeopardize their program admission. A caring faculty leader with a 'need-to-know' policy will go far in giving students the confidence to disclose.

Points to consider:

- Medical information should not be a part of the application process. Otherwise, students who are rejected may have legal basis for a claim against you. Always wait until after students have been accepted to get this information. Medication information may or may not be useful.
- If possible, have your campus medical team collect and review the medical forms, and work with them to make sure that proper accommodations are met.
- At the end of the program, it is recommended that you shred all medical forms and information that you may have been given to hold throughout the program abroad.

En Loco Parentis

You have a duty to act in the best interest of your participants. What will you do for a student in case of an emergency if a medical decision has to be made quickly? When you cannot reach the parent, you have to act. Period! As such, you may wish to include a medical surrogacy statement on the medical information form or include this as part of your general release. If you have a 24-hour crisis management plan on your home campus, you can also rely on your health services department to keep health forms on file and make these important decisions.

Points to consider:

- Are you prepared for the responsibility of answering for a student's medical needs while abroad?
- How will your university support you if you have a medical crisis to contend with while you are abroad?

Crisis Management

A crisis is the last thing you want to experience, but it's one of the risks in study abroad. You never know when a manmade or natural disaster might occur, so you must be ready for anything. Does your university have a crisis management plan that includes international programs? If not, what will you do in an emergency? Never take students abroad with just a hope and a prayer.

Chapter 7 details what a crisis management plan should include and the process of establishing one from the perspective of a case study. Generally, your role is on-site response. You will report back to the campus as the crisis unfolds. Your exact responsibilities and expectations will vary according to situation, but you should know who to contact, and be prepared to report to your administration every detail of the emergency.

Points to consider:

- What is a reportable emergency?
- Who do you call first in the event of an emergency?
- What funds are available and how quickly are they provided to you in the event of an emergency?

- In what situations will insurance assist with emergency response? When will it not?
- What sort of documentation will your campus expect? Will you issue a final written report following the crisis? Fill out a form? Hold a debriefing?

3.8 Disciplinary Issues

It may be understood, but disciplinary problems can occur during study abroad programs. To prepare students for study abroad, your pre-departure orientation should include some warnings about conduct and how students can get a one-way ticket home. Be sure to always inform your participants ahead of time about university policies and procedures.

What are university conduct rules? Do they apply abroad? Find out what your university policy is and abide by it. Also, find out how disciplinary issues can follow students home. Will students answer for their conduct abroad once they return to campus? If this is not written down, advocate for a policy that actions abroad follow participants home. Students need to fully understand how serious and how detrimental their actions can be to other students and to the program at large.

Process

It is certainly possible for you to enforce stricter guidelines for expulsion from your program than those specified by your university at home. Participants on programs abroad are responsible for following conduct rules not only for their own safety but for the safety of others as well. As such, disciplinary action may be taken more quickly on programs abroad, but should always be done in consultation with the home campus. Make sure students know the rules and that your university will support you. Your conduct guidelines should follow a procedure, such as:

- One strike and you're out!

- o   If a participant's safety has been put at risk by another participant
- o   If a law has been broken in the host country
  - Two strikes and you are out!
    - o   If a student has put his own safety at risk.
    - o   If a student has somehow hurt the reputation of the program at the host site.
  - Three strikes and you are out!
    - o   If a student has done something irresponsible that hurt himself only, such as miss the bus for a mandatory activity.

Document all disciplinary action. Have students sign a statement, if they are willing to do so, of what they have done and the warning or any behavior modification expected. Your study abroad office might have a disciplinary report form already established for you to use. Whatever the case, having documentation may cover you in the event that a student decides to appeal a decision once at home, or sue you and/or your university for improperly handling the situation.

A release form should be part of the paperwork process for your participants. If not included in the study abroad requirements you should work with legal counsel to devise such a form. You may also consider building a group contract that you work on with your participants prior to departure. You can discuss openly the rules and behavioral expectations for the program and allow the group, with your input, to create a list of standards through this discussion. As the program carries on you can remind participants that they created the rules for what is not acceptable.

Confidential Reporting
Students want to know that what they tell you will be kept confidential. If they come to you to report a problem with a fellow participant, they want anonymity. They also don't want mom and dad finding out about their problems. How do you balance this

with the need to keep students safe and address possible disciplinary issues? This is especially important for faculty at small town schools where you may already have personal relationships with your students and/or their parents. Just remember that you are obligated to your student's privacy by law.

Every faculty leader has to create an environment of openness and build trust. You do not want, or need, to know the deepest and darkest secrets of your participants, but you do want to be able to handle a dispute before it gets wildly out of control, and help students who are in trouble. Students have to understand that you are there to help them. But what do you do with the information? If a student approaches you with an argument he is having with his roommate, an argument for which there were no witnesses, what do you do? Disputes between roommates can quickly grow out of control, upsetting program dynamics.

In the case of a student who has come to you in confidence, you should inform him or her that you will have to talk this over with the other participant in order to mediate between them. If the confidence involves a personal issue, you may discuss it with the campus study abroad staff, health center, counseling center, or your co-director for perspective. What if a student is talking about suicide? You can be held liable for not reporting student mental health threats. Don't sweep them under the rug; address issues as they arise. Anything that threatens the well-being of an individual must be addressed and handled appropriately.

Reporting to family should not be an issue if your students sign a FERPA waiver on their study abroad or university application. FERPA, the Family Educational Rights and Privacy Act, provides privacy for educational records of those who are 18 years and older. As painful as it is for parents, study abroad staff, and you as faculty leader, details regarding program participation cannot be shared openly.[2] Check with your university to determine what policies exist and whether or not students sign FERPA waivers at the university level.

Case Study

A student was kicked out of a summer program in Europe. The student's group flight ticket was cancelled as he was escorted to the airport for early departure. The student, however, never left. It was later discovered that he was bouncing around Europe, enjoying the remaining weeks of his 'program' when his mother called the study abroad office asking details about the return flight. The study abroad office was stunned that the mother did not know, but was also bound by FERPA regulations to neither confirm nor deny even the participation of the student, much less his disciplinary standing in the program.

- How would you handle the expulsion of a student on your study abroad program?
- Would your study abroad office be able to reveal to a parent or guardian that a student had been expelled?
- Would your administration support your decision to remove a student from the program?
- Would the length of the program play a role in your decision to remove the student?

Common Issues

The most common problems reported by faculty leaders are tardiness, roommate spats, and alcohol-related misconduct. This should come as no surprise to anyone working with traditional college-aged students. Students who break the rules should be sternly warned or penalized. Meeting times on tours should be stressed as well. Students need to know that departure time is the time that the bus pulls out, not the time that they should be

---

[2] For more on FERPA, see the US Department of Education website.

making their way to the bus. That said, there are likely some sites where you cannot leave students behind safely. If there is public transport available for students, leaving a lagging student behind keeps the rest of your group on schedule.

Students who show up drunk or hung-over need to be dealt with immediately. What are your rules for alcohol-related offenses? A student nursing a hangover cannot contribute appropriately to the program and a drunken student will be disruptive.

> On the first day of a short program, one of our students had not arrived by the time we were ready to leave for a tour that was central to our program. We left the hotel and got on our way to the tour without her. When we arrived as a group, she was right behind us in a taxi. Fortunately, it was a lesson for all the students and no one was late for the remainder of the program.

Points to consider:

- What are your university guidelines for disciplinary action at the home campus?
- How will your university support your disciplinary decisions made abroad?
- Can disciplinary decisions abroad be appealed at home?

3.9 The Last Word

You have plenty of responsibilities as a faculty leader, and all of them are important to your program's success. From learning the steps students must take to participate in study abroad, to attending faculty orientation, to handling program finances and logistical arrangements, you will be very busy.

Your study abroad office should have established standards of practice for study abroad, but you may be going it solo or be one of the first to blaze a study abroad trail at your university. If so, pushing through a creation of standards is possible and will be worthwhile not only for you but for those who come behind you. Research health and safety issues for your site and find out how university student disciplinary rules apply to study abroad. You will never regret being prepared for your program or asking the difficult questions at your university beforehand.

Chapter Four: Student-Faculty Relationship

4.1 Defining Your Role: Clarify Expectations

Given the intimate nature of the experience, faculty and students will learn more about each other during a study abroad program than they would in a traditional classroom. However, this casual togetherness can lend itself to a variety of misunderstandings and even unethical behavior on the part of the faculty. This chapter is about building successful and appropriate relationships with our students abroad. It clarifies what students expect of us as leaders and what we expect from them as learners.

You should not be a "buddy" to students, but neither should you be cold, distant, and strictly disciplinarian. The time you spend with students in this much more intimate teaching space simply won't allow it. The goal is somewhere in-between but you must always be seen, ultimately, as an authority figure and competent leader. This does not mean authority only in terms of discipline but on the site and program. If students don't see you as capable, you will lose their trust and respect when you need it most. It is always better to relax from an authoritative position than to firm up after starting as a buddy.

A program abroad is a "campus-in-miniature." You are obligated to either take on roles that are normally assumed by others or act as an intermediary. While it is normal that you would fall into roles such as *resident director* or *parent*, you must be careful to never assume any role that requires a license or certification that you do not possess. For example, when it comes to *counselor* or *physician*, you need to put on your intermediary hat and make sure each student gets what he/she needs from trained experts, either back home (via phone or email) or on location. It is important to effectively balance your roles and responsibilities.

Orientation, which was discussed in Chapter 3, is a great time to set the stage for the students. Address your expectations before you ever get on the plane. What should students call you? What are the academic requirements, conduct expectations, and disciplinary measures for the program? Shedding light on this early will eliminate confusion later on.

Address
If your students have known you by Dr. Smith in the classroom, then continue this mode of address. Leading a group abroad can be stressful enough, not to mention change of intimacy in your teaching space. It's not a good time to create a new buddy dynamic between you and your students. On the contrary, you may need to bring out a new, more authoritative image than previously demonstrated in your traditional classroom.

Academics
Be upfront and clear about your academic expectations. Make sure students understand the assignments, work expectations, grading scale, and institutional policy on academic dishonesty. Dispel the 'vacation' syndrome of study abroad and quickly let students know they do have to complete academic requirements for the program. It's not just a trip; it's a course for academic credit, and it will appear on their college transcript.

Distraction plays a big role in students not taking their courses seriously. An *academic contract* can come in very handy, if done before a program begins. You cooperate with students to develop a game plan for staying focused and doing quality work, and they develop a sense of ownership over their learning experience. Be reasonable and willing to adapt to the situation if needed. For example, if no computer labs or internet cafes are available at your host site, allow hand-written papers or offer a deadline for turning in the final paper after you return home. Requiring a 10-page research paper in a 2-week program abroad is not realistic. However, giving students a post-program deadline to turn in a 10-page research paper, *following* a 2-week program abroad, is not only realistic, but also common practice.

Some of the distraction that inevitably happens abroad can be used as a learning opportunity. Journaling is a good way to bring seemingly random experiences together and provide opportunities for reflective thinking and internalizing. Helping students debrief experiences that are structured and those that are not will go a long way toward their learning and positive assimilation of the experience. Chapter 5 goes into detail about how to foster the learning process in your program abroad.

Emergency vs. Problem

Study abroad is much more accessible than it used to be, giving more access to a varied student body. This means that we welcome students who generally do not step outside their comfort zone, but are willing to do so with their favorite professor. As the faculty leader, you are the primary point of contact for these students, and the one they will call when they need help.

Though students take the initial risk of getting on the plane, they sometimes need a lot of handholding after they arrive. What you might view as a minor problem is actually a major crisis to them. Clarify to your students the difference between an emergency and a problem. An *emergency* is something that requires immediate and active assistance of others. A *problem* is something else that people can usually figure out by themselves.

Whether it is their first time out of the country or their troubles have been exacerbated and compounded by jet lag, culture shock, or language barriers, your students will expect *you* to take care of them. By preparing students ahead of time for what they might encounter, you help them work through difficulties on their own. Include sample scenarios and share problem-solving tips. If you empower your students to think creatively about a problem, you will find that they are more than capable of attacking just about anything that comes their way.

No matter how seemingly minor, you should still assist students who think they have problems, and keep a journal. Being able to refer back to the 'who, what, when, where and why' of program mishaps will help you not only with possible liability issues, but also with program planning in the future. Learn from others and your own experiences so that in future orientations you can give real-life examples to students of emergencies versus problems and strategies on how to handle each.

If you plan to be abroad for any length of time with students, you can expect to run into both problems and emergencies. While you are responsible 24/7 for handling all student issues, you cannot be everywhere at once, so the better you prepare your group to handle minor problems on their own, the more rewarding their experience will be, the more personal growth students will experience, and the more sanity you will retain.

Points to consider:

- Keep in mind that what students call you abroad (Dr. J or Joe) will follow you home to your campus classroom.
- Do students know when they can call and wake you up and when they cannot, if it's not emergency related?
- Do students have the means to reach you at any time?

4.2 Building Credibility

You start building credibility with students, and people in general, from the moment you meet them. Be transparent about the program. If you do not know the answer to a question, you should never wing it or pretend that you do, since being wrong can cost you much more than your credibility! Instead, tell students that you'll find answers to their questions. You are working through many details to gain the knowledge that you will need to competently design, plan, and implement your program. Give students the confidence that you can do this, even if it's your first time.

On campus and while abroad, you must continually earn and safeguard your credibility as a competent and trusted leader. There are many ways that you can do this, from promotion and orientation to the completion of a program, successfully replete with all that you promised students from the beginning.

A professor co-leading a short-term study abroad program in Eastern Europe had expressed concern over the potential challenges he would face in dealing with alcohol consumption by his students. He came up with the idea of having everyone in the program (students and faculty) sign a pledge not to consume alcohol while they were abroad. So, everyone signed this pledge during the pre-departure orientation.

After arriving on site, the two professors and students met for an opening dinner in a local beer hall. During the dinner the professor who had initiated the pledge, ordered a beer. Soon everyone was partaking of beer and wine and telling stories as if they were at a fraternity house. Vows were broken, seemingly with the approval of the faculty leaders, and students were drinking a lot. This quickly escalated to oversleeping, which caused students to miss morning classes and hold up group excursions.

Within the first week, the same professor became more and more frustrated with the group and began to isolate himself, often leaving students to wonder what was happening the next day in the program and forcing his colleague to take on additional responsibility to keep the program moving forward. He expressed contempt for the students in general to the point of lashing out inappropriately at them.

As a result, the two professors never worked together again, and the program was less than successful academically, logistically, and in every other way.

Promotion

Do not promise anything that you cannot deliver. Activities are never set in stone, and are always subject to change, until they are over and done. If you promise activities that do not pan out, students will be disappointed and could lose respect for you. Your first opportunity to build credibility is when you promote your program truthfully. Whether at your campus study abroad fair or through a presentation to your class, this is a great opportunity to set the stage for a successful program abroad.

Use the word *tentative* in your promotional materials and in your discussions with students. If an activity is a possibility but not officially part of the program, present it to the students in just that way. Then, it will not appear as though you did not deliver on a promise, if it fails to come through. When collaborating with another faculty member, co-develop fliers and agree upon talking points for presentations. It's easy for a first-timer to become so excited about an upcoming program that a little wishful thinking plays a part in marketing. At best, this may annoy students who chose the program based upon your illusion. At worst, you could lose all credibility with students and their behavior towards you may reflect this loss. Students may even want their money back.

Chances are good that some of your participants have not traveled abroad before. Be prepared, helpful, and open to questions and concerns; no matter how irrelevant or even foolish they may seem to you. Students will probably have questions about scholarship availability, optional travel before or after the program, how this will help their future careers, if they need to know the language, if there is good shopping, if their host family will have cats (because of allergies), potential hot water schedules, etc. Do not be dismissive of questions or unprepared to offer satisfactory answers. Students may be turned off if you are dismissive or leave them with a sense that you don't know what you are doing or care about their concerns.

Sell not only the program, but also the possibility of a greater, longer experience in the country, and perhaps region. The bottom line is that you need a certain number of students to meet budget goals. Some may only be recruited to go with you by your ability to sell them on things outside the boundaries of your program, such as opportunities for independent travel afterwards.

I was contracted by an institution to develop a program abroad for a particular department. One of their faculty members who had been teaching the first part of a course online, prior to the entire group meeting on site, had made claims to students about how they would be treated by locals, cultural issues, excursion options, housing, and restaurants, all completely different from the reality on-site (and the printed marketing materials we had developed together). This was done without my knowledge, and I did not learn of it until we all met on site for the first time. Needless to say, some students were displeased with the true nature of the program and phone calls were soon coming in from parents. Thankfully, some students were great and found the reality to be a good challenge. I was able to smooth things over and get us through the program but the faculty member had lost all credibility with his students. Everyone thought him incompetent at best, a liar at worst, and within a week, he was taking no part in the program outside of his classroom.

Orientation and Course Meetings

Another ideal opportunity to establish your credibility and role as a trusted, competent leader is during pre-departure and on-site orientation and/or course meetings. How the group sees you and chooses to relate to you begins here. This is also key to winning trust and establishing yourself as the leader.

Always say what you mean and mean what you say. If you tell students you are available every evening in the lobby for certain hours, but they arrive during those hours and you are nowhere to be found, then they will lose faith in you. Be open, honest, and allow students to place warranted trust in you, your knowledge, and your ability to lead the program abroad.

> Not only does the faculty member have the opportunity to impress upon the student her level of expertise in the content area and with regard to traveling at the destination, but she also has the opportunity to bring the students into the mix, allowing them to make suggestions, ask questions about the content, logistics and giving them a sense of ownership over the program.[3]

Providing students with a sense of "ownership" helps to proactively meet their need to feel some control during what can be a stressful period. Students can feel a major loss of control abroad, even helplessness, and may be excessively reliant upon you.

Prepare students for the unexpected and how it might affect a planned group activity, like a public transportation strike during a city excursion. Help students understand that activities may be altered due to reality, as opposed to lack of planning.

Points to consider:

- Have you been open and honest with students, and yourself, at every step of planning and implementation?
- Have you prepared your students for the unexpected, and the need for them to be flexible at all times?
- Have you fostered a sense of trust from students by answering, or finding the answers to, their questions? Alternatively, have you empowered them to seek out answers and report back to the group?

---

[3] Interview with John Stauf, Director, Center for Global Engagement, The College of the New Jersey, 15 April 2010.

4.3 The Intimacy of Teaching Abroad

Given the lack of personal space on most study abroad programs, you may find yourself thinking of students as friends. This can come back to bite you if you're not careful. Generally speaking, don't take part in social activities together that you would not take part at home. Don't confide in students or talk about things that you would not talk about in a domestic classroom. Be vigilant, keep things in perspective, and do not say or do anything that everyone, especially those in authority on the home campus, cannot know about. You will have little choice but to get to know your students better, just keep things in perspective.

It is natural to want to blow off steam, but using your students for that purpose is unprofessional and may even cause a rift among them, accompanied by a serious loss of respect and authority for you as their teacher. When a student irritates you and you discuss that with another participant, or even with your co-director in an earshot of others, you are entering into dangerous territory. Some think naively that confiding in one student will increase their respect and likeability. It does not. It can and will backfire. Guard yourself, and your credibility among all students.

> On a short-term program, a faculty leader confided in a male student about the irritating nature of several female students. The male student initially found it to be an exhilarating bond. As the program progressed, however, he felt burdened by this 'secret' and tried to keep a distance from the faculty leader.

Students are not your friends and cannot be your dates. Anytime a faculty member pursues such a relationship on a study abroad program, it puts your program, your students, your reputation, your career, and your university at risk. It also exposes you to unnecessary legal liability. What if the object of your affection does not return your advances? You may have signed a statement when you were hired agreeing to sexual harassment policies at your institution. As such, you can be fired for these unwanted advances or sued by the student for sexual harassment. Other program participants may feel that you are partial and they are being dismissed and/or neglected while you cultivate a romantic relationship. Your role is to care for *all* of your students ethically and professionally. Remember your role.

Though you may be smart enough to guard against developing an intimate relationship with a student, you may need to guard yourself against a student's desire to develop a more intimate relationship with you. Given the closeness of the group, and that many students feel somewhat helpless while abroad, it should come as no surprise that a student may become infatuated with a faculty leader. You never know what your students are thinking and who might be interested in you. As such, don't put yourself at risk of being misunderstood. Never have a student in your hotel room alone; watch what you say and how you compliment students, and don't play favorites, as other students are keen to pick this up and resent you as a result.

> In one program, a faculty leader is known for playing favorites by secretly sharing information about more "authentic" shops and restaurants with (typically male) students that he likes. He does not share this information with students he does not like.

Points to consider:

- Do you have a tendency to be overly friendly with students? If so, how will you create personal space that keeps you from becoming too intimate with them?
- Do you have a way to blow off steam without confiding in students? Create a communication system for yourself before you leave that does not involve students.
- Is your program structured in a way that you can safeguard against being alone with students?

4.4 Traditional College Students: The Millennials

You are probably already familiar with the varied qualities that make this generation unique. Millennials are an interesting mix of being entitled, suspicious, narcissistic, nurtured, protected, and stressed.[4] Although they may require more planning and handholding throughout the process of study abroad, the good news is they are interested in going abroad and are more global-minded. They also have a strong commitment to service, which is helping to make service-learning programs among the fastest growing in education abroad experiences.

Millennials are capable of many challenges that go with improving the planet. "Whether it is teaching English in China or building a well in Africa, Millennials are 'in tune' with global needs" said Phillip Gardner of Michigan State University.[5] College-aged students that travel or study abroad often do so again through volunteer programs. Paradoxically, there is a consensus among educators that this generation does not trust itself to make responsible decisions. Setbacks include hovering parents as well as enabling university cultures that tolerate extended adolescence.

> The products of hovering, nurturing, protective parents, this generation will be a conforming, risk-averse bunch, respectful of authority yet demanding that it deliver on its promises...Millennials might be more emotionally fragile and demanding of attention to their stress-induced psy-

---

[4] For interesting and sometimes conflicting discussions on Millennials, consider Neill Howe & William Strauss *Millennials Rising: The Next Great Generation* (2000), Jean Twenge *Generation Me: Why Today's Young Americans Are More Confident, Assertive, Entitled--and More Miserable Than Ever Before* (2006), and Vanessa Van Petten "What Kind of Kid Do You Have? The 4 Types of Millennials" (*Radical Parenting*, 2010).

[5] Andrea Stone, "'Civic Generation' Rolls Up Sleeves in Record Numbers." (*USA Today*, 19 April 2009).

chological needs, less interested in the act of learning than in the results.[6]

> Some universities attract a large percentage of students who are interested in volunteering abroad or taking part in short-term "missions" with hands-on experience. Mission-minded students tend to pay more to take part in short-term, 1-2 week, projects for no credit than participate in a month-long study abroad program that can earn up to 6 credit hours. Creating service-learning programs that fuse both academics and goodwill may work very well if you have the right market of students.

Nurtured
Typical millennial students have always been praised and treated as important. They crave attention and have come to expect frequent positive feedback. When traveling abroad, they could be shocked to find that others in the host country do not find them to be as special or interesting as they find themselves. Students at the extreme end of the spectrum experience a lack of focused attention when away from the family members who have praised them continuously. When coupled with feelings of loneliness they may be less vigilant of their own safety, and more susceptible to predators. Scheduling feedback sessions with students individually can give them the reassurance that *you* are available to focus on them, even if for a short few minutes.

Entitled
Typical millennial students have no qualms about asserting their views. They want to convince you of their potential—not because they respect you and want to prove themselves but because they feel a sense of entitlement to your respect. They are highly optimistic and expect to receive high grades and *attaboys* from their investment in education. They anticipate that things will go their

---

[6] Barrett Seaman, *Binge. What your College Student won't Tell You*, pg 279 (2005).

way and if they do not, then a parent will often step in or encourage them to push harder to get what they deserve. You may also find that your prevailing campus culture has added to this mindset, making your job in study abroad much more difficult. Traveling abroad can be challenging for those students who feel wholly entitled, because they are not always going to get what they want and need, *when* they want it and need it.

Protected
These students have been sheltered and protected by their parents, from the difficulties of growing up. Naturally, they expect that faculty and staff will also resolve their conflicts and ensure they are safe. This is why spelling out the differences between emergency and problem is very useful. Do not be surprised if at first you are continually on call. Consider it a weaning process but take time to make every situation a teachable moment. This will help your students grow their own support systems, which will serve them well in to the future. Remember, for someone to be successful they first need a challenge. In the millennial world, success has always come naturally for just showing up.

Narcissistic
Millennials often possess an overabundance of self-love. They are sure that they are already perfect, and so, focus on getting good grades more than on learning. They, and their parents, are more typically concerned with GPA and extra-curricular activities as a ticket to higher paying positions and success. However, if you build in opportunities for small, daily programmatic success, the learning process will be ingrained. Students may be completely focused on ordering that first meal in Hungarian—with their limited vocabulary—but you know they had to memorize the words and anticipate responses to do it. If they did not know they would succeed, they would not have tried, and if they failed, it would not have been their fault.

Stressed

Millennials often feel pressure from parents for success and have been pushed to balance athletics, academics, and multiple activities. The use of new technologies has been engrained nearly from birth and this has helped students become exceptionally good multitaskers (although results may be lacking in quality). This generation, supposedly, has experienced less free time than any before it. They are accustomed to and perhaps are more comfortable with structure. As a result, their ability to effectively manage free time abroad may be limited, and could constitute a challenge that they are reluctant to face. This, in turn, may result in little cross-cultural, academic, or social learning. Too much unstructured free time may be detrimental to their health.

> A successful program pairs US students with Ukrainian students from the local community. Within a week of working together, much of the free time students have is spent, by choice, with their new partners. Cross-cultural learning takes place, students become more proficient in the "other" language, and health and safety measures are greatly increased.

Poor program planning can set students up for failures that are out of their control. Though you do not want to artificially praise anyone or make the experience too shallow and easy for authentic learning to occur, you should assist students in finding real daily accomplishments. A frustrating day filled with jet lag and perhaps homesickness can be turned around by a student making his first successful purchase in the native language. Such seemingly small successes can play a large part in a cross-cultural program. Ensure that there are opportunities for success over and above the classroom and service projects, and plenty of debriefing.

Suspicious vs. Unfaltering Loyalty

On one hand, millennials question everything and are not impressed by rules or authority. On the other hand, they may be respectful and blindly follow your lead. Both of these extremes make it difficult to piece together pre-departure requirements. How can you expect students to follow rules that they treat as bendable and breakable? On the same token, how can you expect students to take initiative (especially for their own safety) if they follow like sheep? Ultimately, a student's learning, health, and safety are his or her own responsibility. Enforcing the rules of the program, while simultaneously helping students make some of their own decisions, is key.

Tech-Connected

Many students are used to communicating daily with their parents and friends. Thanks to cell phones and the Internet, this probably won't change much while they're abroad. Removing students from their home campus and the physical proximity of their support networks will not remove their connectedness to home. It may not affect the student's desire to have their parents involved in the program abroad, and it may also not hinder the parent's desire to make decisions for their student while away. The Millennial student has been raised "collaborating and socializing in a virtual world without borders."[7]

> A parent called during a field trip to tell me that her daughter was not feeling well and asked if I could get her medical treatment. The student was with me all day, even at that moment, and never said a word directly to me about how she was feeling.

Obviously, some programs, depending upon the location, may preclude internet access or the use of cellular phones. Students opting for such a program probably know well in advance what to expect, and may have even selected the program specifically for this reason. But in other areas of the world, there are expectations of staying in regular contact with people at home. Building

---

[7] Paul Gallagher, "The Challenge of Tech-Savvy Millennials" (*Human Resource Executive Online*, 12 Mar. 2010).

time into the program that will allow for connectedness (i.e. the arrival call to tell mom they are safe) will help to alleviate anxiety. Of course, you can still make contact rules, such as no cell phone usage during class time or excursions.

Helicopter Parents

Parental involvement can manifest at any or all stages of the study abroad process, from the initial decision to go (or not) to follow-up communications after the program is over. Helicopter parents don't allow their sons and daughters to make their own way, their own decisions, and their own mistakes. These students are encouraged, by their parents, to seek exception to the rule, as if the rule doesn't apply to them. Helicopter parents have taught these students not to make their own decisions and never to fight their own battles. For every meeting with a student of a helicopter parent, there is a corresponding phone call from the parent.

An advisor found the following note attached to a scholarship application, from a parent to her student:

Mary,
To apply for the scholarship you will need the application, a financial statement, essay, reference letter, and a transcript. Your financial statement is all ready to be picked up in the Financial Aid Office. The essay prompt is why do you want to study abroad and what will it do for your academics and chosen career. To get a transcript, you must go to the Registrar's Office and request it. You will have to pay $3 upstairs at the Cashier's Office and then bring your receipt back to the first floor for the transcript. Then take that, along with your other documents, to the study abroad office by 4:30 today. I'm sorry that I can't do this for you.
Love you,
Mom

4.5 The Last Word

While this generation of students can be challenging, they are also adventurous and oriented towards service. They like and want to help others, and they'll get on the plane. They come with more mental health issues and other baggage than ever before, as well as hovering parents. Being treated as another participant will remind these students that they, too, have to follow the rules in order for the program to be successful. If given the chance, you may find that these students experience greater growth after having challenged themselves to cut back their extensive connections and step out of their comfort zone. And who knows, those baby-boomer parents might learn a thing or two as well.

Chapter Five: Student Learning Abroad

While tying your course to location is a critical first step, there is more to student learning than program structure. The next steps implore us to foster depth within the structure that we create, to cultivate student-learning outcomes.

5.1 Goals and Assessment Models

All programs need to have measurable goals for student learning. How else will you, your students, and the administration know that the program was successful? Program evaluations typically deal with student satisfaction, but we also need to think about student learning as it relates to each program's stated purpose. Let goal creation be a first step to planning. Having goals in mind before beginning the program development process will keep you focused. Goals should be clearly stated and all planning flow from them. Your program can then be designed to meet those goals to the greatest extent possible.

Few faculty leaders think about, let alone write down, assessable goals. Nonetheless, if you are creating a syllabus to the standards of your institution, then there should be some stated goals for your program and course. The step that is frequently missed is the intermingling of goals with the program and itinerary. Your program justification should *not* be "this is the program I want to do and where I want to do it." Sit down and think about what you want your students to learn and why it can and should happen in the location you have chosen.

For more on outcomes assessment for education abroad, consider *A Guide to Outcomes Assessment in Education Abroad*, edited by Mell C. Bolen. This guide explains what should happen in a study abroad program, and what should manifest in students. Students should gain insight into course material, critical thinking skills through host-country exposure, learning strategies through host-culture integration, language communication skills in the host country, an increased ability to recognize cultural differences, greater respect for diversity among people, and an awareness to compare cultures and critique one's own value system.

Learning goals will also help you plan the logistics of your program, if you establish them beforehand. For a two-week program studying Habsburg architecture, does it really make sense for students to stay with host families? For a Russian language and culture program, does it contribute to learning goals for students to room together in hotels or stay with host families? Would it be different for a service-learning program? Or a rain forest ecology program? Different learning goals guide different logistics. Let these goals assist your planning.

Course Idea: Photo Journaling

Students with a camera, in a different country and culture, will be taking photos constantly. Have the students narrow down a day, week, or month's experience into a single snapshot. Each student then explains, in so many words, the "who, what, when, where, and why" surrounding that moment and its meaning to them. This exercise slows down the experiential overload, allows for reflective interpretation, and helps students to internalize their experience in a deeper and more relevant manner.

If, like many others, you are in a situation where financial support for site visits and program planning is extremely limited, then you may need to have programmatic, academic, departmental, and professional development goals in place before submitting your proposal. Study abroad programs are not only for your students; as we discussed in Chapter 1, they have the ability to enhance your career and your department through the internationalization of curricula. Whether you are competing for university funding, or applying for a grant, having well thought-out, assessable goals will help. Almost always, funding usually goes where it is expected to have the greatest productivity.

After you have established learning goals, determine how you will assess them. You may certainly use quizzes and exams for the purpose of study abroad assessment; however, try to be creative and seek out new or alternate measures. Opportunities to exhibit conversational skills in real situations, effective cultural interaction, and student initiative in cultural events or activities are all worth measuring, especially if your program is based on language and culture. Study abroad assessment will and should be different from assessment that takes place on campus, and should match your program's learning goals.

5.2 Turning "That's Weird" into Teachable Moments

It is your responsibility as the faculty leader to move students beyond what they think is negative or 'weird' into true understanding. Pay attention to your students. Listen to what they say to you and each other. Intercept the possibly destructive comments that can pop out instantly. Lead students beyond the idea that everything they are seeing and experiencing is strange and unusual and transform the moment into a learning experience. You can do all of this and more by taking time to debrief experiences with your students, as they occur.

Often the comments that reveal a lack of understanding are not meant to be hurtful or derogatory toward the host culture. Debriefing exercises allow you to move negative feelings into cultural comprehension. Be thankful when a participant is willing to speak his mind rather than internalize it without understanding. Encourage discussion that allows students to talk about how they really feel, but not within earshot of natives. No one wins if your host partner university overhears a discussion about how disgusting your students find the food.

> On the last day of a study abroad program in Asia, a participant said, "I can't wait to get home where everybody speaks English." One of the directors of the program overheard this comment and quickly steered the students past their negativity and into a level of understanding. He did this by saying "Now you know how international students feel when they come to our campus."

Facilitating a discussion of differences is welcome and okay. Do not ignore that there is discomfort associated with living amongst the 'different' and acknowledge the legitimate discomfort your students may feel. You have the ability to bring things into perspective for students so they can move past the negative connotations into understanding and empathy. Never be afraid to have REAL discussions. Always look for these opportunities.

5.3 Challenging Students

Your students are willing and able to face challenges. In fact, they may have already faced challenges in their decision to finance the program, negotiate with unsupportive parents (or spouse), and juggle work obligations. Even their decision to take on the unknown is a huge challenge faced and overcome. As international educators, we can help students by putting them in awkward situations for which we've prepared them. With our guidance, students can successfully experience some emotional, physical, cultural, and social discomfort (not pain) that is instrumental to our learning goals.

> When facilities aren't as comfortable as they are at home, we can remind students that if the natives can *live* in a certain manner, then surely students can *experience* it for a short while. The goal is to overcome, or at least, tolerate. Being out of one's comfort zone is a part of learning to adapt, exercising cultural sensitivity, and developing a self-awareness of cues that we give to others.

Many students from faith-based institutions have come to expect continual spiritual support on the home campus. If this is your institution, you may find that students expect you to tend to their spiritual needs through Bible study, prayer meetings, and finding local church services for them. Tell your students in the orientation how much assistance in this area you will be providing once on site. Should your program be training for future mission work, it could help students to navigate short periods of spiritual "dryness." Learning how to minister to one's own spiritual needs, or develop a new group with strangers, will be of great value to their future, wherever it may take them.

5.4 Participation

Your students are going to feel like fish out of water, at least for the first few days, due to jet lag, the new group dynamics, and culture shock. This may affect how they participate or feel capable of participating. Beginning with the pre-departure orientation, discuss the expectations with regard to open participation. Define the various aspects of the program: homestay, language instruction, cultural events, program goals, assessment methods, and how participation is valuable to their learning experience.

Participation is not the be-all end-all of student learning, even while abroad. However, students need to feel free to contribute openly. If students are unwilling to participate for one reason or the other, consider using individual feedback sessions as open opportunities to talk. This technique has been successfully used by domestic faculty working with foreign students on US campuses. Depending upon one's cultural background, open questioning and class participation may be extremely uncomfortable, so private conferences are substituted into the student's participation grade.

Open-ended questions poised to individuals reluctant to participate, leaves them in a comfortable position to answer. "How did you feel about the dinner last night?" is a much better question than "Why do Ukrainian dinners have three obligatory toasts?" It allows students to explain their feelings without worry of being right or wrong, and it promotes discovery and discussion. Likely, someone in the group will ask about the toasts and if it is normal to have three of them. You turn student questions into teachable moments and promote active participation.

Although we have discussed student disciplinary issues already, it is worth noting that you must state your policies with certainty. Student absences, non-participation, lateness, and even drunkenness can wildly affect your program and spin it out of control, if you have not clarified early on what the consequences of these behaviors will be for students.

5.5 Intercultural learning
Most faculty-led programs don't have the structure to accomplish cultural assimilation goals. However, what we can and should accomplish on all study abroad programs is the development of intercultural competence that makes our students effective in adapting to new places and cultures.

What helps to develop intercultural competence is an open mind and willingness to lose the judgmental baggage that can't come with it. Your goal should be to provide students with tools, starting with the pre-departure and on-site orientations, which will help them to effectively navigate and adapt to the environmental and cultural challenges. There is nothing gained by the shock value of a new situation, which can make your students recoil. They may never, in their entire lives, forget an awkward cultural experience on your program, but is that real learning?

Pre-experience coaching, of which orientation is the first part, is a way of prepping our students for what they will see, do, or join. Informing students of what they should expect and why it will happen is a crucial piece of program readiness. This extra attention to detail will keep students from judging or recoiling. With a good sense of what to expect, students pay closer attention, look for differences, learn more throughout the program, and participate in a culturally appropriate manner. For true intercultural learning to take place, we need to create a desire in our students to watch, listen, and be curious about local behavior. This type of activity requires that you, the coach, be well versed in the cultural norms and that you have evaluated and can explain the experiences in a judgment-free manner.

Advance coaching, done correctly, does not take away from the challenge of the experience, it gives your students the tools to successfully navigate the situation and build competence. Coaching our students to negotiate difficult or simply different situations creates resiliency, the ability to adapt, and a greater sense of self-worth. That said, it should be clear that prepping students for a packed schedule and cultural differences is altogether different than telling them every detail of what will actually take place. Be careful not to steal the mystery of the experience.

What if you do not have all the answers? Sometimes, taking a group of students abroad is like babysitting kids. Not that they are childlike, but there is a constant stream of "why this," or "why that," or "how long." You cannot be expected to answer all questions about cultural traits, history, politics, or the time it takes for the train to be repaired before you can be on your way. Common questions can be delegated to the students themselves, to gather the answers and report back to the group. Having students find and interview a local about a particular item can be an excellent cross-cultural experience that is assessable for grading purposes. Again, it is more than acceptable not to have all of the answers.

Empower your students to discover for themselves, and maintain the element of wonder and mystery by not spoonfeeding them.

5.6 Fostering Respect for the Host Country

Observe, interact, learn, serve, and be an ambassador for your country. Especially with service-learning or mission programs, students and faculty often come from the point of view that *they* need *me*. Students on all types of study abroad programs, frequently spout words like 'weird,' 'strange,' and 'bizarre.' They are not trying to be disrespectful, but they may need your help to improve their attitude and language.

Study abroad is not a vacation. Students who want to look around the area, take photos, and go home should not study abroad but instead join a tour company and go on a trip. You are not leading a trip but rather a study abroad program. Therefore, you must assume that when students sign up, they are interested in more than just the seeing buildings and pressing the buttons on their cameras to haughtily show everyone where they've been.

In the case of service learning or missions, we assume students have a *heart* for what they are doing. As faculty leader, you must assure that the work to be done is truly needed, that you are seen as *assistants* to a sustainable initiative rather than do-gooders coming to change things or repaint a school for the third or forth time that summer. The positive intercultural learning that goes on with students and locals working together ensures that both sides can maximize the experience. It can also serve to motivate, instill organizational skills, and leave a spirit of servitude that will sustain a project or effort when you leave.

Even for short-term study abroad, students can exhibit a spirit of learning and respect for the intercultural possibilities that exist. Students housed in hotels can take the time to talk with the desk clerk and maybe discover that she sleeps downstairs every other night to help the hotel while her five-year-old son is staying with his grandmother, which is an hour away by train. Asking "why" can reveal how similar we are; for example, most of us work hard and sacrifice to provide for our families. Lessons can be found at every turn if we just take the opportunity to discover them.

5.7 Trusting Students for Independence and Free Time

You have to foster your own trust in students. There is only so much handholding that you can do to herd the students along in completing an academic task. You also cannot be everywhere at once shepherding them as if they were toddlers. At some point, you need to let go and let them drive their own learning experience, even if their driving is poor.

Academically, you can format your courses so that students are required to accomplish specific tasks on their own as part of their overall grade. Your pre-departure orientation should spell out the course requirements completely and give students a clear understanding of in-class and out-of-class work that will be required. An academic contract signed by participants may help to clarify the time expectations for outside work.

Do not forget the importance of the time students spend outside of class, and what it brings to the academic experience. Outside learning on education abroad programs is typically thought to be of greater 'educational' value than class time. Individual assignments augment learning and students can complete them on their own throughout a given period. Such assignments might include attending local religious services, visiting any variety of museums, going grocery shopping, interviewing an elderly person, peer or faculty member, and even going to the movies.

Journaling after each experience is a tremendous way to assess each student's use of their time, and to keep them on target. You may implement daily guided journaling, whereby you provide different questions every day for them to answer. Be careful with your instructions. You do not want to end up reading the personal and deep-dark secrets of your students. Be specific about what sorts of things should and should not go into their class journals. Recommend that the deep-dark personal journaling be done elsewhere, as this journal is only for the course.

No matter how well you orient the students, a part of the learning experience is making choices, and for better or worse, they will make choices on their own—some of which will get them hurt, in trouble, or in a few sad cases even killed. Making choices builds self-confidence and independence, because it gives students a sense of power over their lives. You should foster their independence and help them to make good choices, but be prepared if they do not. They will probably fail from time to time and need help and guidance along the way. This is all part of growing up.

> On the second week of a study abroad program in Budapest, I broke my collarbone after running and tripping over railroad tracks. This was no one's fault but my own. The program director could not have foreseen this happening and did not warn us not to foolishly run across tracks. Providing warnings for every eventuality would require a month-long orientation of "what-if's." You too, as faculty leaders, cannot expect to know every possibility of harm that can come to your students, especially from their poor choices. Nonetheless, you need to immediately assist with finding medical assistance afterwards. Be prepared.

5.8 Debriefing the Program: Unpacking the Experience
The program does not end with the flight home, or at least it shouldn't. Students often do not understand or fully feel the effects of their experience abroad for weeks or years to come. It may be months down the road when a student realizes he has a changed attitude about differing religious beliefs and is finally able to correlate it to interaction with people he encounters in his travels through Turkey. How can we help our students with the unpacking of the experience once we have returned?

Immediate Reflection
If you have built in a post-program project for students to complete, it will help them with immediate reflection on the program. If you do not have a post-program report or final course meetings following the program, you may wish to pull students together under the guise of an informal gathering. You can still use that gathering to review what happened and how students are handling their return home. Guiding a response to the overall program (be it written or oral) can help them break down what just happened. What was challenging and why? Were they surprised at what challenged them? How do they want to incorporate or not incorporate pieces of the study abroad experience into their lives? How will the experience affect their future?

Students who participate in longer programs often have adjustment difficulties coming home. What happens is they arrive with unrealistic expectations of jumping back into routines and realize quickly they have changed and the things they used to do at home are no longer interesting or accessible. These difficulties can be lessened if they are coached for their return. Providing guidance before they leave and after they return can help students successfully unpack the experience that they had over the course of a semester or more. It can help to motivate them again in a place that suddenly feels mundane. Be sure to look at the fantastic resources for guided re-entry listed at the end of this book.

Long-Term Reflection
Long-term reflection is something you, the program administrator, may never know about because it will be happening in lives of your former students long after the program has concluded. However, it is important that you know as faculty leader that your interactions with students abroad will inform this later reflection. Your depth of debriefing, and how you have prepared them to come home, can shape how they view the experience (positive or negative) in the long-term.

5.9 The Last Word
Goals and objectives should be key drivers in the academic and logistical planning of your program. They can help you articulate what it is you not only *want* to do on-site, but *need* to do in order to make the program a success. Goals will differentiate your study abroad program from an international *trip*.

Assessment methods should be creative and developed to meet specific learning goals. Home-campus assessment tools cannot usually be successfully transplanted to education abroad programs without several adjustments and modifications.

Remember that student experiences and learning outside of the classroom are just as relevant as in-class learning. Coaching, as opposed to strictly teaching, can deepen the student's learning experience and cultural competence.

You can provide your students with the tools to successfully complete the program. Foster your own trust in them to succeed academically and make good choices.

Debrief the program with students as they prepare to "unpack" the program and prepare them for internalizing positive memories and experience.

Chapter Six: The Study Abroad Office

The study abroad office is a critical, first step for higher education institutions to responsibly, and effectively, support international study, work, and/or travel. This office provides oversight of risk management policies and procedures, proper student application screening, and faculty-student orientations, among other things. If you are new to study abroad, or you don't have the support of a study abroad office, this chapter is for you. It will help you to understand, advocate, develop, and/or build a study abroad office to support faculty-led programs.

6.1 The Proposal Form

Every faculty-led program should begin with a form that clearly outlines the course(s) abroad, delves into program logistics, and articulates faculty knowledge and expertise as it relates to the proposed international location. Below are the components of a well-constructed proposal form.

Faculty Information

- **Contact Details** – Ask for both campus and off-campus contact information. As programming extends to pre-departure preparation, you may need to contact the faculty leader after hours or during university holidays.

- **University Status-Rank** – If retired or adjunct faculty are not eligible to teach abroad, it should be clearly stated. Ask if the faculty will be on sabbatical in the year leading up to program departure. This is critical since the burden is on the faculty to recruit a minimum number of students, and faculty on sabbatical the year prior to the program typically don't recruit well.

- **Chaperone Minimum** – Does your institution require that a minimum of two university personnel chaperone each study abroad program? If so, this should be clearly stated. The second person doesn't have to be a faculty member within the same department, and doesn't have to be a faculty member at all. This person could be staff or an administrator who is willing and able to join the program for director duties.

Program Information

- **City and Country** – Do you already have a partner operating in this city and country? If so, does your agreement include a "no compete" clause?—meaning you cannot offer other programs there. Are there any other faculty-led programs in this city and country? The answers to these questions will help you gauge the logistical knowledge and expertise that will be needed through the planning stages.

- **Program Dates** – Do the dates fit into one of your regular academic terms? Will special course dates need to be established? Will the Registrar support alternate course dates for study abroad? How will your Registrar support late grade reports for a course and study abroad component that expands across two terms? If the program is offered during the summer term, try to arrange the dates so they don't overlap sessions unnecessarily.

- **Enrollment Goal** – If the course is not interdisciplinary, from where will faculty recruit students? What is the target student population for the course? For example, if the proposal indicates an enrollment goal of 20 students for an upper-level dietetics course but there are only six students majoring in dietetics at your institution, then it is important for faculty to implement a plan to recruit students from other colleges and universities through professional colleagues, conferences, etc.

Course Information

- **Course Approval** – Is the course pre-existing or does it need to go through appropriate procedures for approval? Has the course already been submitted for such approval? If not, how long will this process take on your campus? Is there appropriate time to gain approval prior to the right marketing cycle? If study abroad courses are run under a seminar or other such course number, they many not need additional approval outside of the proposal process.

- **Cross-Listing** – Will the course be cross-listed in another discipline? Or will the study abroad course substitute for multiple courses across disciplines. This is quite helpful for those fields that do not draw a large number of majors. Drawing from two fields or more will expand the recruitment pool and help the program succeed.

- **Course Level** – How will the faculty differentiate between or meet requirements for undergraduate, honors, and graduate-level study? If the course is available for graduate credit, does the faculty teaching the course have appropriate credentials to teach a graduate-level course? Do students need to be admitted to the graduate school in order to earn graduate credit?

- **Degree Requirements** – Does the course earn valuable graduate, major, minor, or general education credit? If it does not fulfill one or more of these requirements, it'll be harder to sell. Your student pool will be limited to those who need elective credit or aren't concerned about credit at all, and you probably don't want that *kind* of student on your program. Faculty must also be willing and able to recruit students from other departments.

- **Course Schedule** – Will the class meet prior to or after the program? Above all, study abroad courses need to meet the academic requirements of your institution. However, having pre- and/or post-program components that either introduce content and/or follow up on what was experienced abroad tend to produce students who are more globally aware. These students also experience less culture shock abroad and reverse shock upon their return home.

- **Course Details** – These details should demonstrate that the faculty leaders take their course seriously, the course is directly linked to the location abroad, and course-related assignments are appropriate to subject matter. You may also ask how each assignment is directly related to the activities of the program, their correlation with each assignment, and texts being considered for the course.

- **Course Link to Location** – What is the advantage of teaching the course at the chosen site? The faculty should be able to clearly articulate the link between the location and the course in a convincing and meaningful way.

- **Language** – Will language be an integral part of program preparation? A language prerequisite should be indicated if the program is located in a country where a foreign language is the official language and the students will need to communicate with natives for project development. Even when foreign language communication is not an essential part of the course, it is accommodating to have some "survival" language training built into the pre-departure orientation or course meetings prior to the program.

- **Intercultural Competence** – Do the program goals consist of intercultural communication, the study of contemporary culture, and/or the ability to culturally adapt? How will these goals be met? Will students have the opportunity to interact one-on-one with locals?

- **Recruiting** – Faculty should clearly indicate their intentions to speak with classes and groups, advertise campus-wide, communicate with professional colleagues to promote their program, and/or recruit through multiple universities, or across the nation. They should have a clear idea of how they are going to reach their intended audience with program information and meet their minimum enrollment goals.

- **Assessment** – Will the students and/or the course be assessed while abroad or upon return? Does the assessment model apply to the program's stated goals and vice versa? Does your institution require that the program be assessed to meet certain requirements for accreditation?

Logistical Information

- **Familiarity with the Program Site** – Have the faculty members ever been to the international site and do they have extensive personal knowledge of the location?

- **On-Site Contacts** – What contacts do the faculty have on site? Will they make arrangements themselves or work with a designated third-party provider?

- **Itinerary** – Do the faculty have a proposed itinerary? Have they proposed specific excursions, site visits, and field trips relevant to the course?

- **Housing** – Where will the participants be housed? Do the faculty have knowledge of local housing options or have they identified a specific accommodation provider?

- **Fitness** – Is there a minimum experience or fitness level? For example, the ability to walk three miles every day or have scuba experience or certification? Consider offering some options for the faculty rather than letting them come up with their own. There is a tendency to *underestimate* the strenuousness of proposed activities and *overestimate* the physical abilities of participants.

- **Health Risks** – Are there known health risks related to either the location or the activities being offered-required on the program? If so, additional university clearance or release forms may be required or students may need to be alerted to mandatory malaria medications, for example. Faculty should know this upfront.

Supplemental Material

- **Curriculum Vitae** – The CV underscores the qualifications of the faculty and should be kept on file indefinitely for program review, as well as for university review should your accrediting body wish to audit your programs.

- **Course Syllabus** – The syllabus should follow normal university guidelines for format and information. This should also be kept on file indefinitely for the same reasons as the CV.

- **Signature Page** – The signature page of the proposal should be signed by 1) the applicant, 2) the Department Chair, and 3) the Dean of the School or College of the faculty. This ensures university support for the faculty members to teach and escort students abroad. It also provides approval of academic credit and assures that program dates won't interfere with each faculty's on-campus duties.

- **Background Check** – If your university doesn't require employees to complete a background check when hired, consider including this as part of your application requirements. Results (inappropriate behavior, violence, serious grievances from students, sexual harassment, etc.) can and have been used to deny a faculty member the ability to lead programs abroad.

At my institution, a faculty member consented to a background check as part of the normal faculty-led proposal process. When it was revealed that the faculty had a long history of theft, the Study Abroad Office consulted its legal counsel, who ultimately denied the faculty member the ability to direct programs abroad. He is permitted, however, to teach abroad so long as another acting director can handle program finances.

- **Tentative Budget** – A ballpark estimate and rough cost breakdown is helpful during the proposal process; however, it is difficult to know actual cost before all the details have been worked out. It is better for the detailed budget to come after the approval process, and you can then provide more guidance on how to research costs and put together a program budget.

Components of the Faculty-Led Program Proposal

Faculty Information
- Contact Details
- Status and Rank at the University
- Department
- Emergency Contact
- Second Chaperone Information

Program Information
- City, Country, or Region
- Dates, Term, or Semester
- Student Enrollment Goal/Minimum Participation

Course Information
- Course Title and Credit Hours
- Course Approval
- Academic Discipline
- Cross-listing
- Level: Undergraduate, Graduate, Both
- Degree Requirements
- Course Schedule
- Course Description and Content
- Syllabus
- Assignment Details
- Course Link to Location
- Language Preparation
- Prerequisites
- Intercultural Competence
- Recruiting
- Assessment

Logistical Information
• Familiarity with the Program Site
• On-Site Contacts
• Itinerary
• Housing
• Fitness requirements
• Health Risks
Supplemental Material
• Curriculum Vitae
• Course Syllabus
• Signature Page
• Tentative Budget
• Background Check

6.2 The Proposal Process

The first step in the call for proposals is to decide on either a rolling or a firm deadline. The advantage of a rolling deadline is that faculty can develop programs at their leisure and propose programs closer to the time of departure. On the other hand, this opens the possibility of receiving a proposal far past the regular student application deadline or receiving a proposal so close to the student deadline that it deters adequate recruitment.

A firm proposal deadline allows the study abroad office to maintain a progressive timeline for review, development, and recruitment. While many offices have a fixed proposal deadline, they may also accept and review proposals earlier. This extra time is especially useful to faculty members who have never created a study abroad program, allowing more time for development and a greater duration and flexibility for recruitment.

The annual call for proposals should be widely advertised. Ways in which you can spread the word to faculty include:
- University newsletter
- Intranet announcement
- Fliers for campus mail
- Department and university websites

- Emails to Deans and Chairs with a request to forward an invitation to each faculty member in their department
- *Teach Abroad* fliers and brochures placed around campus and sent to faculty at the beginning of the term or year
- Faculty champions announcing the call for proposals and spreading the word in their departments
- Information sessions each semester, providing sample program itineraries, budget worksheets, and proposals
- Use of international committee structures to alert faculty
- One-on-one targeting of faculty who have expressed interest in the past

Open information sessions tend to draw faculty who have been considering the option to teach abroad but are hesitant to start the process. For those who have never taught abroad, the application can be daunting. Your session should include where the proposal form can be found, how proposals are reviewed (rubric), and how to complete the process. You should also walk through the process step-by-step and be transparent about expectations, reviewers, and timeline.

An information session will also alert you to new faculty interest. Make it a point to meet each faculty member personally, keep a list of their interests and expertise, and use this information in the future development of ideas and programs. If, in any year, you find a lower number of proposals, or an academic area that is in need of a study abroad program option, you can refer to your list of faculty interest and expertise, and call on select individuals to consider a proposal.

6.3 Alternatives to a Faculty-led Program
Many universities are members of consortia, which allow faculty to teach abroad. Teaching through a consortium is quite different than developing a study abroad program. Consortia may offer more guidance on activities and excursions, make arrangements for transportation, and reserve accommodations. They may also provide a program director to manage logistical and disciplinary issues. Consortia enable faculty members to plug into an existing structure with their only responsibility being to recruit and teach.

They may offer stipends, sometimes greater than compensation for faculty-led programs, and cover additional expenses. Faculty should be made aware of the different level of responsibility.

While you cannot control consortium deadlines, you can promote them within the framework of faculty-led information sessions. Consortia provide a good first step for faculty who need some international experience but have the eventual goal of creating their own study abroad program. There are also, of course, those faculty who never create their own program abroad, but instead propose various courses abroad through consortia. Consortia are a fantastic way to gain international experience without a great investment of time and resources.

6.4 Proposal Review

It's important to consider a committee, rubric, and process for the proposal review, as opposed to an individual making decisions without defined logic. An established committee, made up of both faculty and staff, from different colleges and areas of the university, provides a fair process for the consideration of study abroad proposals. This committee may make *decisions* regarding program approval or denial, or it may only make *recommendations* to a Director or Coordinator of the study abroad office. In any case, it should be capable of providing a critical review, and have the power to request revisions if needed.

Academics

It is helpful if at least half of your committee is made up of faculty members who either have taught on a program abroad, created their own programs abroad, or have significant experience with study abroad consortia. A proper academic review will...

- Ensure appropriate academic rigor for the course
- Ensure that contact hours and course requirements are in line with university policy and procedure
- Ensure reasonable expectations for assignments rendered during the time abroad
- Ensure appropriate connection between the course and the proposed location

- Assess academic needs (additional course approvals and required prerequisites)
- Ensure faculty have sufficient academic credentials to teach the proposed course(s)
- Determine whether the faculty have been approved by their departments

The committee should report their findings: approval, revision recommendations, wait-listed, or proposal rejection. Generally, proposals find their way into the 'revision recommendations' category and few are rejected for academic issues. If your university caps the number of faculty-led programs it can support in a given year, you may find yourself with a waitlist of programs for the future. This is a great problem to have but can deflate faculty members who are excited about their programs *now* as opposed to in the future. In this case, it's important to give encouragement to your "standby" faculty, to keep their interest alive.

Logistics

The logistical review is more heavily driven by the study abroad personnel and other administrators. The following should be taken into consideration when conducting a logistical review:

- Does the faculty member have knowledge and expertise in the location, culture, and subject matter of the program? Has he visited or spent extensive time at the destination? If not, how does he plan to compensate for this lack of firsthand knowledge? Does he/she have the necessary contacts to assist with group arrangements on-site?
- Is the itinerary reasonable? Are there adequate course-related activities? Is there enough free time built into the program? Does the itinerary include adequate time for meals? If there are multiple sites to be visited, are the travel logistics realistic, or should they be modified?
- Is the budget reasonable? Does it clearly state which program components are included and which are not? Are any necessary components missing?
- What are the housing arrangements? Are they reasonable in terms of monetary, practical, and safety concerns?

- What resources will be required of the study abroad office? For example, new faculty-led programs that need help identifying and navigating third-party assistance for on-site arrangements will take more time than those programs in which faculty have established their own on-site arrangements. Are there resources to adequately assist ten of these programs per year? Five? Two?

The committee may recommend that faculty do more homework to ensure local activities meet program goals. A proposal may be held until faculty visit the location (if they've never been there before) to gain a more intimate understanding. High cost may be cause for revision as well. If your students receive financial aid for university attendance, you can probably assume that most will be looking for a reasonable price. Having the right student audience and marketing plan is critical for recruitment.

Acceptance or Revision
Proposals can raise many questions and may only be the starting point. Faculty-led veterans will have no problems completing a proposal form with all the necessary details that merit approval. However, those new to the process will need more guidance that possibly results in waiting another year. The committee review structure should allow and encourage guidance from experienced faculty leaders and the study abroad office.

Depending on your office dynamics and mission, you may want to set a limit on the number of faculty-led programs. Perhaps you don't have the capacity to manage any more programs abroad or there are multiple proposals fishing from the same pond, leading to fewer programs meeting their recruitment goals. In any case, it is important to have a solid basis for acceptance, rejection, or revision of proposals and a strong sense of university goals for study abroad. If your university is more focused on the assessable outcomes of study abroad, then it's probably focused on long-term assimilation rather than short-term faculty-led programs abroad. In this case, a limit on the number of short-term programs is advisable. If your university has participation goals that are more number-oriented, short-term faculty-led programs can surely help, especially if participation levels in your long-term programs have leveled out or if funding is an issue for students.

In the review process, committee members look at various aspects of the program proposal to help ensure its success. Because faculty-led programs are high maintenance, it's crucial for faculty to understand the time commitment. Having a frank discussion about faculty responsibilities for program recruitment and management will hopefully weed out those who are not fully committed to the work involved. Through these discussions and open meetings with interested faculty, there should be a process of self-elimination for those who do not want this level of responsibility. Some will choose instead (or be asked by you) to propose courses for consortia or accompany already customized groups abroad without teaching. These customized programs are usually organized by the study abroad office and facilitated by a host institution abroad. In any case, it is important to have a sense of faculty commitment before investing your time in a program.

Revisions may take many forms, from syllabus and assignment recommendations to activity time allotment. A syllabus for a 4-week island program is altogether different from a syllabus for a split course that starts at home and finishes abroad. Assignments may vary from instructor to instructor, and from field to field, but practicality is the key. If computer access is limited, then it's not practical for students to type journal entries. The committee may recommend they be hand-written instead. Having 2-hour lectures in addition to class excursions and group dinners, every day with no free time, is unrealistic and will tax students (and faculty) to their breaking points. In this case, the committee may recommend more free time and less classroom-based lecture.

It is important when communicating committee recommendations back to the faculty members that the study abroad office make very clear which revisions are required, if any, for acceptance of the proposal, and which revisions are otherwise optional. Using words and phrases provided by the committee and signing the correspondence 'on behalf of the committee' is very helpful, especially when referring to academic components of proposals. Since the study abroad unit is an administrative one that often does not consist of academicians, committee support is crucial in bridging the gap between administrative and academic requirements necessary to develop quality programs abroad.

6.5 Faculty Proposal Acceptance

After a proposal is accepted, faculty should meet with the study abroad officer in charge of faculty-led programs. This can be done through a group meeting or one-on-one and must be scheduled to accommodate all faculty who are leading programs abroad. Yes, this meeting should be required of all new program leaders, but also of those who have led programs before. If they are unable to attend, then other reasonable accommodations should be made. The purpose of this meeting is to go through the many processes and procedures for program development and student recruitment, answer any questions they might have, and make sure the study abroad office and faculty are on the same page.

The program development and recruitment process begins with student advising. It is important for faculty to understand where students are coming from and how to get them involved in study abroad. First, faculty need to understand everything from application to financial support to obstacles that students face. Students generally do not know the level of experience that faculty leaders have in study abroad, but often assume they have all of the answers. As such, it is important for the study abroad office to inform faculty about the student processes and procedures, so that faculty are equipped to assist students through the process or at least point them in the right direction.

It is helpful for the study abroad office to create a flier template for faculty to modify with their program information. The flier should include information like program dates, course details, course registration information, faculty contact information, financial aid and scholarships, contact information, application guidelines, tentative program itinerary, on-site housing and meal information, travel guidelines (i.e. are students required to fly together), and cost breakdown. This template enables the study abroad office to provide standard and consistent information to students interested in a variety of programs.

Components of the Post-Acceptance Faculty Meeting

Student Advising
- Application Process
- Scholarships and Financial Aid
- Recruiting Responsibilities

Program Development
- Budget Creation
- Itinerary Development
- University Processes-Paperwork for program finances

Dates and Responsibilities
- Orientation Dates, Agenda, Responsibilities
- Course Details, Credit Policy and Requirements
- Required Faculty Paperwork

6.6 Student Application Process

What is the student application process? Can application components be altered by the faculty member or is there a standard application packet? Is the application online? What is the deadline? Does the application require the student to obtain approval to participate from an academic or other adviser? Does it require any supplemental materials? How are applications reviewed and considered for acceptance? These are all questions that faculty need to have answered before they can advise students.

The application and method of review should be standardized, if possible. A complete application usually consists of an informational form, an essay requirement, a university transcript, and a reference letter. Additional components may be added to some programs, such as personal interviews or language proficiency tests. Different admission requirements are also necessary for programs, and may include some or all of the following: minimum GPA, prerequisites, physical fitness such as the ability to hike for five miles at a time, or logistical-academic abilities.

After a decision is made for application requirements and applications are received, what happens next? Is there a committee to review applications in conjunction with the faculty leader? How are notifications sent to the students? Faculty leaders, particularly first-timers, will need to know how to screen student applications for their study abroad program. The following general guidelines, customized to fit your university, should be explained to faculty as they navigate the student acceptance process.

- **Review** – The review of applications should be conducted by a committee, and the committee should include study abroad personnel and faculty leaders of the program abroad, among others. This structure is especially helpful for new faculty who don't know what to look for and look out for in applications.

- **Transcript** – At home, the grade point average is usually a good indicator of academic success; however, it may not be as important in study abroad. Students who thrive in a domestic university setting may find it much more difficult to balance independent coursework abroad. On the other hand, students who are academically average at home may thrive abroad with an alternate course structure. The selection committee should consider the following points in their review process:

    o What is the cutoff for good academic standing at the university? This should remain the minimum for acceptance into all study abroad programs.
    o Will students be enrolled in a university abroad? If so, they must meet the GPA standards for enrollment at that university.
    o Does the transcript indicate a pattern of dropping and adding courses or of taking courses at least twice to receive a passing grade? These students may find themselves failing courses or lacking pre-approved courses or credits when they come home.
    o What grades has the student earned on the home campus in similar courses to those he/she is planning to take abroad? If a student is taking a history course in France but his history grades have been C's and D's, this should be considered by the committee.

- **Essay** – Most study abroad programs require an essay, which indicates why the student is choosing the program and how he sees himself applying the experience to his academic and career goals. Such an essay is usually quite telling. If a student applying for a semester program chooses not to focus on how coursework will affect his degree program, but instead on fun in the sun and his buddies who encouraged him to apply, you should see a red flag. Maturity is a serious consideration when reviewing applications and the essay can help you determine a student's readiness to study abroad.

- **Application** – Is the application complete? Did the student indicate the courses he wishes to take on the program abroad? Have all questions been answered? Is the application signed? Has anything been crossed out by the student and is there any vital information missing?

- **References** – Some referees provide clear, student-specific letters and others use a generic template. So, a letter may or may not be an indicator of student success on a study abroad program. Alternatively, you can ask your referees to use a set form that you provide with very specific questions.

- **Notifications** – Notification of acceptance or denial may fall on the study abroad office or the faculty, or both in cooperation. It's always warmer when the notification comes from the faculty leaders as opposed to the study abroad office. The important thing is to clarify who will be responsible for this task.

- **Interview** – If a student has a borderline GPA, you may be able to assess his academic commitment through an interview. An interview may lead to a better understanding about hurdles and requirements for support. An interview may also serve to facilitate agreement among the committee.

6.7 Student Financial Aid
Faculty need to understand the financial aspects of their program abroad. One of the first questions students may ask is how much the program costs and if there are scholarships available. Without becoming an expert in federal aid or scholarships, faculty should

be able to refer students to the appropriate resources. This begins with some basic terminology.

- **Federal Aid** – Federal grants and loan money is available for higher education, including study abroad. The process of applying for federal aid begins with the student and his parents completing the FAFSA form which is online at fafsa.ed.gov. Because aid is based on educational expenses (tuition, room, board, etc.), students may be eligible for additional funding, if the cost of their study abroad program is higher.

- **Study Abroad Scholarships** – Scholarships may be available specifically for study abroad through the department or university. Faculty should be made aware of these scholarships and applicable deadlines. If you do not have a scholarship brochure, think about creating one. If your office has a limited budget, consider listing scholarships on your website or creating a flier that will direct students who wish to apply. Try to make yourself aware of available national scholarships. For example, students interested in critical-need language programs may apply for the Boren scholarship. Students receiving a Pell Grant are eligible for the Benjamin A. Gilman.

- **University Scholarships** – Students who have university scholarships may be able to use them to study abroad, but policies differ from institution to institution. One university may allow scholarships to travel with the student to all programs, one may only allow it with select programs, and another may not allow it at all. Especially at public institutions, transferability issues are often beyond the university's control. Faculty need to know your university policy and how it affects their students. Which university scholarships are allowed to travel with students? How are they applied to the student account or program fee? If scholarships are not allowed to travel with the students, can the students use them toward a future term at the home institution?

If your financial aid and scholarship process is complicated, consider offering workshops each semester for students, parents, and faculty. Your workshops should cover policies, application procedures, and tips to becoming a stronger candidate. Include financial aid and scholarship personnel to assist with the workshops. These folks can provide additional details to students and families who need clear and accurate guidance.

6.8 Effective Recruiting
It doesn't take a genius to effectively recruit students; it takes strategy and effort. The best form of student recruitment is the faculty dedication to a program. If a faculty member is not well established on campus, he may find himself only recruiting from his courses. However, multiple recruiting tools are necessary to be successful. Marketing panels (with experienced faculty leaders) are helpful to newcomers. See Chapter 3 for tips.

More than anything, students need to be reassured. Far too often, students think that study abroad will cost too much or delay their graduation. They don't find the right fit for their personal and career goals or don't think they're competitive enough for scholarships. Students need to hear from someone they trust that they can and should study abroad. Faculty are the motivation behind students that often gets them on a plane.

After a faculty member saw the price for an affiliate program he proposed to teach, he assumed that students would not be able to afford it, and thus decided not to recruit. Unfortunately, he didn't communicate this to the study abroad office or he could have been assisted with recruiting strategies for an expensive program. The key to assisting faculty is letting them know that you are available, and covering these kinds of issues in faculty information sessions to help ensure their success.

6.9 Transparency
As with many aspects of higher education, transparency in study abroad is important. Most universities have visible policies and procedures that govern just about every aspect of their operation. The same is true for study abroad. While these policies may not appear in a handbook or on your website, they should at least be made available to those who ask. If you have the ability to put

them on your website, or otherwise make them more accessible to the greater campus community, then by all means do so.

It is also helpful for future personnel and faculty leaders to know when specific decisions were made, and by whom. Keeping an internal record of which key players were involved in a policy decision may assist future staffers who are facing challenge to a policy. Don't underestimate the importance of written records. They will only help as the office, responsibilities, experiences, and programs grow. If you make any changes along the way, be sure you have good reasons for doing so and document them.

Faculty need to know the current policies and procedures. Everything from the student application process to program expulsion will concern your faculty, whether they know it or not. If you do not already have policies and procedures included in your faculty handbook or online, it's never too late to start. Begin with whatever you have, adding more information and details over time. Guidelines are continuously evolving, and never complete, but eventually, they will at least be comprehensive.

6.10 Faculty Orientation
Orientation is an excellent way to reach all faculty leaders at the same time. Faculty attendance, on the other hand, is a bit tricky. If you cannot require attendance, then try to make it attractive by offering food, having former faculty leaders on the agenda, or including a letter from upper administration, which encourages participation. Whether or not you can require attendance, it is important for faculty to get the information somehow. You can request an appointment or send the information by email. If you send information, have them sign something that states they have read, understand, and agree to abide by it.

Faculty were still planning programs outside of the study abroad office despite my pleas with the administration and the faculty themselves. Since all study abroad scholarships fall under the purview of my office, I made the decision to withhold scholarship support from students who participated in 'rogue' faculty-led programs that had not been developed in accordance with the health, safety, and academic guidelines of the institution.

Scholarship support denotes official university approval, which is not granted to programs that operate independently.

Faculty Orientation Components

Faculty orientation should include information on policies and procedures as they pertain to health, insurance, safety, resources, crisis management, conduct, liability, and more. The depth of your orientation depends on the amount of time available. Some faculty will come in with questions, but most will not know what to ask. When can a student be expelled? What is the class attendance policy? How does one manage student drinking? Faculty need to know clearly what their responsibilities are and what they are expected *not* to do. They need to be supported and empowered with the confidence to make tough decisions.

Faculty Orientation Agenda

A. Why are we doing this?
B. Some Issues to Consider
    1) Student profile
    2) Technology
    3) Expectation of 'getting what I paid for'
C. Intimacy of the Teaching Space
D. Student Learning and Expectations
    1) Help students debrief their experiences
    2) Give students time to process privately
    3) Teach culture, customs, academics, appreciation
E. Your Responsibilities
    1) Teaching
    2) Student affairs
    3) Logistical issues
    4) Medical and emergency
    5) Finances
    6) Respectable, responsible relationships
    7) University policies
    8) Disciplinary issues
F. Health and Safety
    1) Insurance
    2) Release form signed by students

> 3) Transparency in planning, informing students
> 4) How to help students abroad
> 5) Mental health issues
> 6) Safety resources for program planning
> 7) Emergency procedures
> G. Legal Issues and Liability
>   1) Alcohol usage
>   2) Negligence
>   3) Due care
>   4) Professional liability insurance
> H. University/Study Abroad Office Support While Abroad
> I. On-site Orientation
> J. Return
>   1) Program reporting
>   2) Financial reconciliation of program
>   3) Program debrief
>   4) Student evaluation

Documentation

Consider requiring faculty to carry a small notebook with them, to document issues as they arise. They won't remember details of the illness, theft, or conflict unless they take the time to write it down in the moment that it occurs. This notebook is turned in to the study abroad office at the end of the program, before debriefing. The study abroad office then has a written record of issues that students are most likely to complain about or expound upon in their program evaluations. This handwritten record of events can also prove useful should there be legal action down the road.

Health and Insurance

What is expected of faculty if students encounter health issues while abroad? Common illnesses like the flu and nuisances such as diarrhea and constipation can get out of hand if left untreated. What are other common illnesses? How do faculty assist students who have medical problems abroad?

Faculty should identify a medical facility on-site that can be used for routine care and have a plan for emergency care, should the need arise. If you require your faculty leaders to be CPR certified, then obtain a schedule of the local Red Cross offerings for CPR certification and alert your faculty as soon as possible. Requiring faculty to seek out region-specific health information is valuable in ensuring they are equipped with the on-site knowledge necessary to inform and lead students abroad. It also shows *due diligence* in planning.

Your faculty may know nothing about culture shock. Taking them through the stages from honeymoon to acceptance is vital to their own understanding of what their students may be going through. Some ability to differentiate between culture shock and depression is also important. Invite your health services or counseling director to faculty orientation to discuss common mental health challenges that traditional college students face. These offices may offer help and services to students while they're abroad.

> On a short program to London and Dublin, there was a student complaining of a toothache. Multiple times, I offered to find a dentist for the student, but he was adamant that he could wait until he got home. Two days before the program ended, his tooth broke into pieces. I called several dentists in Dublin who could not take the student until we would have been in the air heading home. After hours of searching, I located one dentist in the area who was willing and able to see him. The student got to the dentist, and he was up and running by the last day.

If your university requires a specific insurance plan, you should talk with faculty leaders about coverage, services, and how it all works. Patients will either be expected to pay for services on site, keep receipts, and seek reimbursement when they return, or the insurance company may offer a *direct-pay* service to the doctor or hospital where the student is being treated. Direct payment is quite helpful, but is usually not available with pharmacies.

Points to consider:

- What are the reporting requirements to the study abroad office or home institution?
- Can the faculty member call the student's emergency contact during a medical crisis?

- What medical information will the faculty member have regarding each program participant prior to departure?
- Is there university-mandated health, evacuation, or other types of insurance? What does this cover?

Safety

What safety-related issues has your institution faced on study abroad programs? Regardless of your answer, the same things that could and do happen at home could also happen anywhere else in the world. So, preparing faculty for this fact is necessary. Not every program goes off without a hitch. Faculty cannot afford to be naive to the fact that safety and health incidents may hinder the student experience as early as day one.

> On the first night in London, a female student went out to a bar with other friends on the program. The friends decided to head back to their residence and left the female student there with a local male she had met earlier that evening. The faculty leader heard from campus safety officers the following morning that the student was attacked and mugged on the street in the middle of the night.

Provide faculty with some scenarios and case studies that bring to reality some of the things that could and do happen to students during study abroad programs. Get them thinking, asking questions, and talking to each other. Then, help them walk through the steps of how to handle each situation correctly. When faculty are informed, and enlightened, they will usually be proactive in considering the safety of their students. A little paranoia can go a long way to keeping people safe and healthy abroad. Contacting local sources, to ensure housing and transportation safety, is an important part of making the program successful.

> One year we flew to Cancun and drove students by bus across the Mexico border into the town of Corozal, Belize. The Overseas Security Advisory Council (OSAC) had given us recommendations on the time of day to travel. Based on those recommendations, we went ahead with the plan, and arrived without a hitch.

Information is critical to fostering successful study abroad programs. Faculty need to know where they should and should not go in the surrounding area, as well as how and when to travel. If they don't know these things already, you can provide them with resources to assist their investigation. If they arrive on-site and only then determine there is a safety issue, they need to know they can still move and/or make changes to the program. Empower your faculty to be as diligent about student safety as they'd be with the safety of their own children. En Loco Parentis.

Points to consider:

- How do faculty scout out which areas are safe and which are not at their site?
- When can and should faculty move their locations or alter planned activities?

Crisis Management

What happens during an emergency? How has your university planned for crisis management in study abroad? If your university or office has not undergone strategic crisis response planning for study abroad programming, we highly recommend you do this sooner rather than later. See Chapter 7 for more details.

Points to consider:

- What constitutes an emergency, real or perceived?
- How is your office notified when an emergency occurs? How much communication is expected with your office and university during an emergency abroad? Does it depend on the nature of the emergency?
- Who needs to be notified in case of a student emergency? How does this change according to the different types of emergencies? How does this change if the emergency pertains to a faculty member? When do you *not* need to be contacted?
- What is the chain of command and level of responsibility for all parties involved in the emergency?

- What is the level of responsibility expected for the faculty leaders during a medical emergency?
- When will an emergency affect program continuation?
- Are refunds available if a program is cancelled abroad?
- Who will pay for individual emergencies? For program-related emergencies? For national emergencies?
- How are courses and grades affected by an emergency?
- What records should be kept? How detailed should you be in your recordkeeping?

> While at a conference, I received a call from a faculty leader who had missed a flight home from China with his six students. He wanted guidance. So, I called my one colleague who was in town and able to assist me over the Memorial Day holiday. I asked for help locating a hotel for a domestic layover the group would have to take. He promptly took care of everything we needed and communicated with the faculty leader.

Conduct

The conduct of some individuals in the group can greatly influence the impression of the program on others. If a faculty leader's attention is constantly being pulled away from program activities and responsibilities to deal with a disruptive student, the program can derail. You should make your faculty aware of both the common causes of disciplinary action, so they know what to look out for and address in orientation, as well as what their parameters are for disciplining participants.

The most common causes of disciplinary action are alcohol and drug-related behaviors, roommate disagreements, and habitual tardiness, or failure to attend program activities. Students may show up for class or an activity with a hangover or may not show up at all after a late night of drinking. Perhaps your application process did not weed out the student who is not serious about the 'study' program, resulting in distractions such as talking during tours or disappearing altogether. Roommate issues always surprise faculty leading short-term programs abroad, since students are not in their rooms very much in a day. But those short hours can provide sufficient time to note painful discrepancies in sleep patterns, hygiene, and personal space issues.

Points to consider:

- Do students sign a release form that pertains specifically to conduct abroad?
- Does the university support a 'three strikes and you're out' policy or can faculty leaders be more discerning for individual programs?
- What sort of documentation is needed when enacting disciplinary sanctions?
- How are disciplinary incidents reported to the home institution? Do they become a part of the student's permanent record?
- In what case is expulsion from a program acceptable and necessary? Do you have any examples of past expulsion decisions? What happens to the student's grades and program fees in the case of an expulsion?
- Does your office require that faculty discuss expulsion decisions with your office prior to enacting them? It is recommended that big decisions like this one be taken in consultation and accord with the study abroad office.

Helping faculty work through what is expected, how your office will support them, and their decision-making is crucial. Unfortunately, poor conduct is not limited to students. Faculty or staff can disrupt a program just as much as students can, if not more so. Some of the same issues you may experience with students (excessive drinking, habitual tardiness, sexual harassment) may occur with co-leaders and program staff. Be ready, willing, and able to frankly discuss the situation with your co-leader or staff, report it to your administration, and take immediate disciplinary action if necessary.

A veteran of faculty-led programs would pick students to take out to dinner once each week. At the end of the 4-week program, there was only one student who was not asked to dinner by the faculty member. The student's evaluation revealed that this fact

> colored his entire experience. He knew the faculty member did not like him, expected a poor grade in the course, and planned to change his major so he would not have to take classes from the same professor again on the home campus.

Faculty should also recognize their own limitations. For example, if they know they cannot keep up with the NASCAR pace of their students, then breaking group activities into separate days or allowing students to meet them at the location of an activity is a good idea. Otherwise student and faculty tensions may rise.

It is also advisable to remind faculty of the university's policy on sexual harassment. How does this policy apply to a study abroad program? You might consider asking all faculty and staff that will be traveling with students to sign a statement of understanding with respect to the policy.

And, finally, what is considered reportable in regards to faculty conduct abroad? To whom is it reported? Is anything considered actionable on the home campus, by your academic department, Chair, Dean, or the Office of Equal Opportunity? Spell out these policies and procedures for faculty leaders.

> When directing a program together with a faculty member who had diabetes, I soon discovered that he was not taking care of himself and his illness. As early as day one, he was neglecting to eat and starting to swell. Nevertheless, he was determined to keep up with his students. After it was pointed out to him that he could be putting not only himself but also the experience and safety of the students at risk, the faculty member agreed to re-structure his course and schedule regular meals for himself.

Liability and Legal Issues
NB: This section should not be considered legal advice and should not take the place of advice offered by an attorney.

When considering liability and legal issues specifically in regards to your programs abroad, consult with your university attorney for policy development and even faculty orientation. If your university does not have an office of legal counsel, then you may choose to retain or consult an outside attorney to address legal issues and advice for your faculty.

Lawsuits are prolific, and study abroad is no exception. In determining what the study abroad office needs to make faculty aware of, consider the following:

- Information and standards on health and safety abroad with respect to the program location
- What marketing materials say and what students have been told will be part of the program
- What student and parent expectations are in regards to care and safety while abroad

As you build your program, keep in mind that you may recruit students who have disabilities, and if so, you should find a way to accommodate them. Mobility International (www.miusa.org) is an excellent resource and help. The laws that govern access and disability can be a little tricky, but in a nutshell, you cannot deny an otherwise qualified individual solely on the basis of a disability (Section 504 of the Rehabilitation Act). The Civil Rights Act of 1991 extends the American Disabilities Act (ADA) of 1990 to US employers in overseas facilities. This means it does not apply when the program abroad is not operated by an American university, but it does apply to American university overseas programs taught by American faculty.

The Family Education Rights and Privacy Act (FERPA) has set limitations on what anyone in higher education can provide to family members of students. FERPA protects students and their records from those who are not in the circle of "need to know."[8] Most universities, especially publics, define 'need to know' in the strictest sense. Even parents who are paying the bills for their students are not allowed access to student accounting and aca-

---

[8] For more on FERPA, see the U. S. Department of Education's website, www.ed.gov.

demic records. As such, your legal counsel may advise that you not even confirm to a parent that a particular student is, in fact, participating in a program abroad. Inform faculty of your university's expectations in regards to talking with parents.

A student attacked on a program abroad decided not to call her parents to share the story of what had happened. She informed her sister that she was attacked, but provided no further details. The parents called the university study abroad office and asked for more information, but keeping in line with FERPA, the university staff were not permitted by legal counsel to confirm or deny that such an attack had taken place.

There is no shortage of legal findings in higher education, though few exist in education abroad. Most litigation in higher education is civil and tort related, pertaining to injury, loss, or damage. Any choice faculty make for their program could result in a lawsuit: housing, transportation, activities, etc. The point is not to scare faculty, but to make them aware of what they should consider when taking on a faculty-led program abroad.

Introduce faculty to negligence and due care, through foresight. What are the foreseeable risks associated with your program, activities, and location abroad? What would a reasonably prudent person say and do in a particular situation? If the faculty leader accompanies a group of students to a pub in London, and then leaves the fully intoxicated group at the pub while returning to the hotel to sleep, what types of risks are reasonably foreseeable in this situation? Oh, let us count the ways....

Let's say some students were attacked outside a pub where the faculty member left them. A lawyer could easily argue that these students thought they were under the care of the faculty leader. After all, he was in the bar with them, and watched them drink excessively. They chose to drink because they felt protected in the faculty leader's care, and they might not have drunk excessively had they known he was leaving early. He unexpectedly left early despite the foreseeable risk. A subsequent attack outside of the pub, then, could be seen as a result of faculty negligence.[9]

Negligence consists of four components: duty, breach, injury, and linkage. When there is linkage between a breach of duty and an injury, a faculty member can be found negligent. As defined by the courts, we have a responsibility to train, supervise, maintain equipment, and warn of impending danger. This means we must actively seek out available information such as that provided by the Center for Disease Control, Consular Information Sheets, US Department of State Travel Alerts/Warnings, etc. This "reasonable care" is indispensable to warning students about possible dangers that should be known by group leaders. When duty is not adhered to, it is considered a breach that can result in injury.

Contrary to the advice provided through guidebooks and tourism websites, a faculty male leader told a female student that a particular market in a more "authentic" area of the city was "safe" to explore. The faculty member had been there many times with no problems and based his advice on his own experience. The student found the market in a depressed and rundown area, rampant with prostitution and strip clubs. Being young, alone and obviously foreign, she received unwanted and even frightening attention in the form of comments, gestures, and being followed. She quickly dismissed the idea of going to the market and took the first taxi back to her apartment.

Faculty leaders should never guarantee anything is "safe." This claim put the faculty leader and his institution at risk of a lawsuit. More importantly, he potentially put one of his student's lives in jeopardy. We can never know what will or will not happen to our students. All we can know is the reasonable risk and this should guide our care of students for which we are responsible.

Not only should faculty be transparent in their knowledge of safety and location issues, but they should also confront issues when necessary. Ignoring an issue in the hopes that it will go

---

[9] For more, see Peter F. Lake's "The Rise and Fall of In Loco Parentis and Other Protective Tort Doctrines in Higher Education Law," *Missouri Law Review* (1999).

away, or because everyone is getting on the plane to return home the next day, will not remedy the matter. In training faculty to lead programs abroad, we must insist that they are prepared to handle student affairs issues if the situation arises. They do not have to handle them alone, but they should be equipped to make decisions and enforce them on-site. You cannot do this from your office half a world away.

What you say you are going to do, you usually have to do, unless the situation changes and it becomes dangerous to continue with the same plan (i.e. a state department travel alert or warning). The faculty leader said he is heading back to the hotel to prepare for the next day's activities and tells the students to call him when they are ready to come back and he will be happy to meet them at the pub and ensure they arrive back safely. The students call the faculty leader but he is asleep and does not hear the phone ring. The same result: students are drunk and subsequently attacked outside a pub where the faculty member left them.

When an incident involves two students, and both feel wronged by the other, what is the process that should be followed? Who handles it? Is your office consulted by the faculty leader? If a policy has been broken, be sure to follow due process. Due process is a systematic approach to making fair decisions; it safeguards the rights of those who have been accused. How do you define due process at your university? Who is involved in determining the response to a situation abroad?

A student claims that his roommate is stealing money from his drawer. Without due process, the faculty leader decides to separate them. He allows the "problem" student to stay in the room alone, and moves the student who complained into a room with other students; the logic being the "problem" student won't be a problem anymore. However, the student who was moved is now angry and demanding a partial housing refund. He feels that he is the one being punished, now in a room with two other students.

Risk exists on practically every level and in every activity with a group abroad—some inherent to the program, some signed up for and agreed to by students, and some unexpected by participants.

Flying is an inherent risk. By nature, students know they will fly on an aircraft to their destination abroad. In the case of additional program-related risk involved with high altitude, mountain climbing, rappelling, horseback riding, scuba diving, etc. legal counsel or the study abroad office should craft a supplemental release form that spells out the additional, foreseeable risk that students will assume as part of the program.

If the risky activity is not related to the course, then it should not be included in the program. There is no reason why horseback riding should be included in a Spanish language program. On the other hand, horseback riding may be a valid and important part of an outdoor education experience. Generally speaking, all of the programmed activities should be related to the course. Otherwise, students should be doing them on their own time and money, or have the option to opt out and not pay for the organized activity. Be aware that injuries and death incurred by sky diving or bungee jumping are often excluded by insurance companies.

Be proactive in obtaining knowledge, and share it. Ask faculty: what do you know, when did you know it, and did you pass it on to your participants? Program information comes to faculty in multiple ways: first-hand experience, third-party provider assistance, US Department of State, US Embassy or Consulate, and on-site reports from natives are a few. Any faculty leader who discovers health and safety information as it relates to the site, or a specific activity, should pass it along to students.

If a student is dissatisfied to the point of feeling wronged, he may choose to take legal action against you and the institution. There are generally four reasons why courts may validate a claim and get involved in an action: (1) deprival of due process; (2) invidious discrimination; (3) the denial of federal, constitutional, or statuary rights; and (4) unreasonable, arbitrary, or capricious action. After you have informed faculty of the university policies and procedures, it is in their hands to adhere to them. It probably goes without saying, but following your own written policies— policies that have been approved by your campus administration and legal counsel—will help keep you out of hot water and help protect you if you land in it anyway.

Student Expectations

Chapters 4 and 5 address in detail the student-faculty relationship and fostering student learning abroad. This needs to be addressed in your faculty orientations. We recommend calling in former faculty leaders to drive these points home. Faculty see the study abroad office as administrative in nature. As such, there are some faculty who will not value your guidance on the academic side of their program, if you do not have doctorate. Allowing them to hear from other faculty who have been in their shoes will strengthen and validate the guidance you provide.

Support and Resources

Faculty leaders need to know that whatever happens while they are abroad, they will be supported. From missed flights and lost luggage to sexual harassment and hospitalization, faculty need the support of not only the study abroad office, but also university administration, to the highest levels possible. Therefore, the last fundamental component of faculty orientation is 'support while abroad.'

While abroad, a new faculty leader may experience any level of uncertainty, and may need guidance. This may not reach crisis levels, but issues may creep up that require either permission or consultation. What are the resources available to faculty while they are abroad? How accessible are the study abroad personnel and who, specifically, will be the contact? Is there a chain of command to follow? If so, what is that chain of command? What if that chain of command fails?

It is important to have a 24/7 phone number for faculty and students abroad. It is also important to have a network of university resources to assist logistically and financially as well. Will the faculty leaders have university credit cards or cash to assist in case of emergencies? What are the parameters for using those funds? What are the rules for financial reconciliation of a program? What documentation is needed when spending student or university funds? Do you or study abroad personnel have funds to travel at a moment's notice, in case of an emergency?

You should also provide your faculty with helpful planning and emergency resources including the following:

- **SAFETI Clearinghouse** – Safety Abroad First Educational Travel Information www.globaled.us/safeti. This website, a resource of the Center for Global Education at Loyola Marymount University, has become a first stop for study abroad planners. Especially helpful to those new to program development is their Program Audit Checklist, which offers some sample forms and useful guidance. In addition, the Center for Global Education offers webinars and co-sponsored workshops on health and safety.

- **IAMAT** – The International Association for Medical Assistance to Travelers www.iamat.org/index.cfm. IAMAT keeps a list of medical practitioners throughout the world that have been licensed in their own country, have received postgraduate training in a western country, and are fluent in English. These medical practitioners have all agreed to a fee schedule established by IAMAT.

- **OSAC** – Overseas Security Advisory Council Osac.gov. OSAC provides a fantastic array of country reports on safety and terrorism and has the added bonus of human response when you email or call for guidance on specific safety areas in a given city.

- **CDC** – The Centers for Disease Control and Prevention www.cdc.gov. Always refer faculty and their students to the CDC for vaccination considerations.

- **Insurance Portals** – Does your insurance provider have an online portal for seeking medical referrals, downloading claim forms, etc.? If so, be sure to provide this information to your faculty leaders.

- **Local Emergency Numbers** – What are the local numbers for police, ambulance, and fire on-site? Where is the nearest US Embassy or Consulate and how can they be contacted?

- *Best Practices in Addressing Mental Health Issues Affecting Education Abroad Participants.* This mental health guide, edited by Barbara Lindeman, is a great resource for all faculty, regardless of their depth of personal experience with mental health issues. Published by NAFSA, the guide can be downloaded for free to its members, and at minimal cost to non-members from www.nafsa.org.

The next chapter goes into detail about crisis situations and how to create a crisis response plan. Faculty who have already used safety resources in planning and preparation are more comfortable when they need them on-site during an emergency.

6.11 Student Orientation
Pre-departure orientation is critical to student preparation for study abroad. It is important not only for students to attend, but for faculty leaders as well. Faculty need to know the parameters you have established for students. What does the university expect of the students? What have the students been told regarding health and emergency situations? How will student activity abroad follow them back to the university, or will it? The details you relay to students must also be relayed to faculty.

Our student orientations are divided into an all-program session and breakout sessions for each program. Faculty attend the all-program portion at least once, but are always expected to lead the breakout session for their program.

Student Orientation Components
In the same room, you will find students who have never been on an airplane mixed with students who have been traveling abroad all their lives. Thus, it is necessary to maintain a balance. Don't spoonfeed the students every detail, but do adequately prepare them for success. Elaborate detail will needlessly lengthen the orientation, and you will end up with an audience that has tuned you out by hour three. That said, there are essential components

to a student orientation that can be covered in the all-program session and program specifics that can be taken care of with the breakout sessions.

All-Program Session

A. **Packing** – Students who have never traveled on a plane before need to understand that there are luggage, weight, and size restrictions, potential additional costs for checked and overweight luggage, and rules regarding what can and cannot be packed in both the check-in and carry-on bags.

B. **Electrical Issues** – What is the voltage/plug configuration abroad and what will students need to operate their electrical devices, without blowing them up?

C. **Departure** – How early do students need to arrive at the airport for their international flight? Let students know that they need to make their goodbyes short, get through the security line, and find their gate quickly. Getting food after, rather than before confirming gate number and departure time is advisable. Students who have not traveled via plane or those whose travel has been completely without delay or incident may not understand how quickly flight information can change, that those changes may not appear on airport monitors, or that international flights board much earlier than domestic flights.

D. **While Abroad** – Students and parents often have no idea how to communicate affordably while abroad. Touching on communication aspects is a vital piece of orientation. Paying the bills, filing taxes, voting, registering for classes, and other practicalities should also be addressed.

E. **Taking Money** – Perhaps one of the more confusing aspects of travel abroad, for those who have never done it before, is how to take money abroad. ATM cards, debit cards, traveler's checks, credit cards, domestic currency, and foreign currency are all forms of funding students have relied on while abroad. Advising participants clearly on multiple means of accessing money seems to be the best way to go. Avoid advocating a specific strategy, but let participants know the pitfalls of putting all of their eggs into one financial basket.

F. **Health and Safety** – This runs the gamut from general knowledge about medication, how insurance applies abroad, and if doctors are available, to sexual activity, not going out alone, and looking for safe havens. H1N1 complications and mental health should be addressed here along with maintaining relationships at home. This pertains directly to the mental health of participants abroad, especially those in long-term relationships. Don't be afraid to get into and address difficult topics.

G. **Crisis Management: Problem vs. Emergency**
What constitutes an emergency? What is the meeting point if there is a terrorist or natural disaster? Who should be called first? Address these details and provide participants with an emergency card detailing on-site and domestic emergency phone numbers. Provide a set of crisis scenarios and divide the audience into groups to discuss these scenarios and share their responses.

H. **Conduct** – Alcohol and drug usage, skipping class, tardiness, and more can be addressed here. What will happen if students receive disciplinary action abroad? When are students expelled? What happens if a student is expelled? What if a student is arrested?

I. **Cultural Immersion** – Culture shock should be the first point discussed here. However, it should be followed by how to prepare oneself to go abroad, knock down stereotypes, get involved in the local culture, and mesh personal and program goals with the location and culture. This is also the perfect place to remind students they are not on vacation but a study program.

Consider offering a parent orientation as well. Parents should be invited to sit in on the student orientation, but there are specific concerns parents have that students do not think about. If you have the manpower to do so, you could pull the parents out of the student orientation before the 'Cultural Immersion' section and have a staff member address the parents separately.

Parent Orientation

A. Introductions
B. Purpose of the Session
    a. Calm fears
    b. Ask and answer questions that you were not allowed with your student during the student session
C. Pre-departure Preparation
    a. For program details, please ask your student instead of calling the office, and he/she can be in contact with the study abroad office when questions remain.
    b. You should be given the following by your student: flight itinerary, copy of passport, copy of insurance card, on-site contact information, front and back copy of credit, debit and ATM cards.
D. Communication
    a. Your student may or may not call you right away after arriving. Why? What is happening on day one?
    b. Using Skype, cell phones, text messaging, emails
    c. Monitor the phone bill to ensure pricing is what you expected or were promised.
    d. Note the time difference.
    e. Daily communication should NOT be expected or even desired. Set parameters before departure.
E. Unhappy Students
    a. Culture shock
    b. Examples of frustrations students experience abroad
    c. Do not offer to solve the problem for your student. Instead, help her remember what she was told in orientation. Who should she call for assistance in the study abroad office or on-site?
    d. Refer to the program handbook when you have questions before calling the study abroad office

F. Visiting Do's and Don'ts
  a. Do not arrive with the student. Your student needs time to get settled without you.
  b. Do not visit in the last week of the program. Your student needs a chance to say goodbye to the program and new friends properly.
  c. Be ready for a role reversal.
  d. Even if you are on vacation, your student is not. She can't skip class to show you around.
G. Emergency Details
  a. At least one parent should have a valid passport.
  b. Know the emergency plan of the program and the university.
  c. Know who to contact at the university if you need to reach your student abroad and you're having trouble doing so.
H. Contact Information
  a. Know how to look up flight arrival information online
  b. Know the contact details of the on-site director
  c. Know the contact details of the third-party provider
  d. Know the Embassy contact on-site
I. Other Practical Concerns
  a. How is your student's program billed?
  b. What does insurance cover?
  c. How are grades transferred?
J. Additional Questions

Program-Specific Orientation

What exactly should faculty cover in the program-specific breakout sessions? It is the responsibility of the study abroad office to help guide faculty leaders, especially those who are new. After a faculty member has led a program abroad and been through this process at least once, he will know better how to proceed and will not need much guidance. For those in their first year, however, a sample agenda for the breakout session is usually welcomed with open arms.

Use the following outline to start, and see Chapter 3 for more information. Breakout sessions should fit the location, the faculty leader, and the details of each individual program. You may have multiple faculty leading programs abroad, and all of them need to provide detailed and thorough information to their participants under each of the following points.

Breakout Session
    A. Travel Details
    B. Logistical Details
    C. Course Details
    D. Safety and Health
    E. Conduct/Behavior
    F. Emergency Response

6.12 Return from Abroad

Upon return from a program abroad, whether it went off without a hitch, found you supporting three separate emergency cases, or was somewhere in-between, you need a program debrief. Several issues should be under consideration here: actual course contact hours, program evaluations, debrief on crises and final response, if needed, and financial reporting. Set an individual meeting with your office staff and all faculty leaders on the program. If necessary, you can schedule additional meetings at a later time to address individual faculty or director issues.

- **Program Log** – Ask the faculty to bring their handwritten program log to you well in advance of the program debrief so you can read it ahead of time. There are some standard questions and issues to address, but inside the logs could be some issues that need wrapping up as well.

- **Contact Hours** – Do you have a reporting requirement for your faculty to detail the total contact hours for the program? If not, check your Academic Affairs unit and accreditation body requirements. It is possible that this sort of reporting could be required in the future if your program is audited. It is better to be safe than sorry and it is much easier to require it now than ask faculty to recall details later. If you have this information on file, you also have evidence that the program is academically sound not only for accreditation purposes, but for any other faculty committee, or university administrative office that may question the academic integrity of your programs.

- **Program Evaluations** – Hold your program debrief at a date after you have had time to review the student and faculty evaluations. You may have a system in which you summarize evaluations or you may just read them for your own knowledge and then pass them on to the faculty leader. In one way or another, the faculty leaders should receive a synopsis. These evaluations should relate not only to program activities, but also to housing, transportation, teaching, and course information. Draw attention to necessary program revisions or improvements that could be made for the future success of the program.

Case Study

Student evaluations revealed unanimously that a highly revered faculty member on campus did not do so well with the group of students abroad. She consistently missed meeting times she had set with the students, led students astray for more than an hour at a time, left students behind despite their on-time arrivals, and put them in danger by asking them to cross busy intersections despite traffic signals prohibiting such crossings.

- How would your office handle this situation?
- How would you handle student evaluations?
- Can evaluations lead to revision of programs?

- **Crisis Debriefing and Final Response** – If there was an emergency during the program abroad, now is a good time for final debrief and response to the situation. Some emergencies are not resolved for months following the close of a program, but the debriefing may be able to serve as your final meeting on the subject. You can discuss what worked and what did not, from the standpoint of the study abroad office, the faculty leaders, the student(s), the location, partner abroad, and home university. You may also have realized in reading program logs that there were a couple of minor emergencies that were not previously reported to the study abroad office. Now is a good time to address those and how they were resolved.

- **Financial Reporting** – If your faculty members carried university cash or credit cards abroad, the debriefing is a good deadline for them to submit any and all receipts and financial reporting. If the financial side of the program requires extensive review, it may prolong your meeting, but it is essential that the faculty leader balance the program's budget and that you see where the funds went, especially if the program account is housed in the study abroad office. Remember that these are student funds and that programs are usually self-supporting. Accounting for the funds now leaves no question later if a program ends with a negative balance or, conversely, with a surplus. Do not be afraid to ask why there is so much leftover funding, or why specific things were not covered that had been promised. Your job is to advocate for the students and be assured that promises to them were kept. You must also be sure faculty understand that going over budget at their own prerogative is not tolerated and will render consequences.

- **Student Issues** – What student issues came up? Did students generally like the pace of the program? Did they complain in unison about a specific activity? Did the faculty find that they should have taken fewer students?

- **Faculty Issues** – Issues can be addressed in two ways. If there was only one faculty leader, you will need to address the issues via your interaction with him/her combined with the student evaluations. If there were multiple faculty leaders, then you should also address the faculty evaluations of each other. This process will be extremely helpful in assessing whether a faculty member should teach again on this program or another, or in determining whether the same faculty should embark together again.

Finally, your office may wish to bring together a program evaluation committee. This could be the same committee that you use to review program proposals. The program evaluation committee would be consulted in difficult cases where your office is seeking input on how to manage an academic issue on a program abroad. If a faculty member has blatantly violated the rules, not only set forth by the study abroad office but also by the university, it can be adjudicated quietly by your office or sent forward to other personnel at your university: legal counsel, academic counsel, a Chair or Dean, or the equal opportunity compliance officer.

6.13 The Last Word
Centralized study abroad offices provide a great level of service to the university as they shoulder the crisis management for all study abroad programs and manage faculty and student training. A comprehensive study abroad office should play the role of liability manager for the university. This office should be empowered by the university to set policies and procedures appropriate to the requirements and concerns of study abroad and faculty-led programs. The synergy of the study abroad office and administration allows for a maximum level of faculty and student support.

Ultimately, your role in the study abroad office is one of support and guidance. Faculty who are new to this exciting process do not know the appropriate procedures for handling students, institutional financial matters, and crisis management in study abroad. It is your job to help faculty create solid programs and follow up with extensive information and support, while they are abroad and upon return. Each semester, as you prepare faculty to develop and lead programs abroad, self-assess to ensure that you are not a hindrance. Remain firmly planted in the role of management and support of study abroad at your university.

Chapter Seven: Crisis Management

Crisis planning, preparedness, response, and management are vital to the success of any study abroad program. Even with the best preventative and response strategies, an emergency situation can creep up at any moment, with outcomes as serious as injury or even death. How such a crisis is handled by the faculty leader, study abroad office, and university can color not only the on-site experience of participants, but also vital relationships within the university. Faculty leaders are pivotal in handling emergencies.

Does your university have a set of emergency protocols in place when things don't go as planned? In today's age of technology, advanced medical care, and insurance availability, it is irresponsible to take students abroad without developing a plan that will guide you in the case of an emergency. Not having a plan in place puts your students at great risk of improper or insufficient care and you and your university at risk of liability. When bad things happen, unpreparedness could be construed as negligence.

So, what is crisis management? What does it look like? It's the process by which we deal with a major unpredictable event that threatens to harm the participants, the university, or the general public. It covers the gamut of harmful possibilities with carefully thought-out, executable guidelines. Consider the following scenarios that can and do occur in study abroad programs:

- Missed or delayed flights
- Loss of Passport
- Hospitalization
- Domestic Family Emergency
- Alcohol or Drug Abuse
- Natural Disaster
- Terrorist Incident
- Political Emergency

- Theft
- Sexual Harassment
- Assault or Rape
- Missing Person
- Student Arrest
- Serious Illness
- Accident or Injury
- Death

Broad plans that differentiate between the 'serious' and 'minor' cases are no longer acceptable. What is serious to mom and dad might not be serious to you, making it critical that we respond to every case with proper due care. Sit down with the appropriate parties to pre-determine and agree upon proper responses *before* your program embarks, as opposed to *after*. It is in everyone's best interest to cultivate a little paranoia and over-plan. If you don't, you may find yourself alone in the event of an emergency. Even worse, you may be named in a lawsuit. If you did something that was deemed as unacceptable, or didn't act when you should have, your university may not represent you or even acknowledge that your program was approved. You must have these discussions beforehand and a written plan in place.

A 24/7 university phone number should be made available to faculty and students abroad. When the call comes in, it must be answered, no matter the time or place and no exceptions. So, who does this at your university? Study abroad staff? Student affairs personnel? University police? Who do you call? Ideally, you will be directly connected with someone who is trained to deal with emergencies and can assist while you manage the crisis abroad. Realistically, however, the first person you reach will probably have to track down the right individual to call you back. Having an emergency management call tree that assigns a clear level of responsibility to different individuals on campus is an important part of the plan. <u>Study abroad programs are a university-level responsibility, not a personal one</u>.

Several international health insurance companies also maintain a toll-free call center to assist students with everything from routine requests to medical emergencies. If your university partners with one of these companies, then faculty and students should be instructed to call them first, regarding medical needs and emergencies. Other companies specialize in international security. Faculty and students just call their nearest alarm center. Staffed by logistics coordinators, security experts, and doctors, these centers provide location assistance, medical advice, and arrange for evacuation in the event of an emergency. In matters of life and death, it's important to act fast! If your university doesn't have the global infrastructure to ensure expert emergency service around the world (i.e. chartering helicopters for example), then consider collaborating with a security services company.

I was directing an annual short program in London with two of our university faculty members and a third faculty observing the program. This program was structured so that as director, I was handling logistical, disciplinary, and crisis issues while faculty were focused on teaching. By the end of day one, I realized I was having a miscarriage at 12 weeks of pregnancy. I was discovered in my room in very bad shape by a faculty member. She called hotel management, secured an ambulance, and ultimately spent three nights with me in a London city hospital as my situation lingered between bad and worse. This faculty member was the epicenter of the management of this crisis for my family and my university as I, the director, lay unable to assist.

- If you, as faculty leader, were asked to take charge of this event, would you be able to handle it?
- What procedures and training does your study abroad office have in place to ensure that all faculty leaders can competently lead or assist in serious emergencies?

7.1 Lessons Learned
This section presents a real crisis and resulting lessons learned, up to and including the creation of a Crisis Management Protocol (CMP) for the university involved.

In the summer of 2005 when bombs were going off in London, I had 30 students either about to leave for, on their way to, or on the ground in London. It was my birthday and I was enjoying the day at home on maternity leave with my newborn. At the time a one-person operation, my university couldn't afford to temporarily replace me. So, a graduate assistant was holding down the fort until my return. It didn't take long before we all realized no one else in the office knew what to do and how to respond to the situation. Nor did they know who was abroad or about to go abroad and with what program or faculty members. I was the only full-time staff person with the knowledge of what to do, and worse, the only one who had easy access to the student information. Needless to say, we were not well prepared for an emergency of any kind, much less a full-fledged, multi-country emergency.

As a result of this experience, when returning from maternity leave the first move was to create, with the blessing of the university administration, a Crisis Management Committee that began to look at emergency situations abroad and determine what the university response should be in a variety of circumstances. This committee consisted of representatives and consultations from the following offices:

- Campus Police
- Legal Counsel
- Academic Affairs
- Student Affairs
- Health Services
- Registrar's Office
- Counseling Center
- News Bureau
- Insurance Providers (on consulting basis)
- Study Abroad Consortia and Program Representatives
- Faculty Leaders from University Faculty-led Programs

Together, they met every week for six months to compose a more detailed and comprehensive CMP. The group identified the incidents that could occur abroad and created a plan that would deal with them if they ever did. It included everything from lost passports to faculty death and everything in-between. In each case, the committee detailed the many aspects of a study abroad emergency: university response, faculty responsibility, logistics, notifications, health, and grading. What resulted was a detailed list of duties and communication plans to guide both faculty and study abroad staff. With a comprehensive CMP that the university developed, it is now clear how to respond to an emergency. The step-by-step manual provides guidance before, during, and after a crisis to faculty leaders on the ground, the study abroad office, and other university personnel.

Though the CMP is written, it is not written in stone. There is always room for improvement. The committee meets annually to review the plan and any crises that took place the previous year. This ensures that the plan still works and provides a relevant opportunity for updates. In the midst of H1N1, it was discovered that aspects of quarantine and its effect on a short-term program really were not addressed in any situational responses built into the CMP. Therefore, the committee reconvened to address quarantine and how to incorporate it into the plan.

7.2 Providing the Plan

Once you have a plan, determine how and what to provide to faculty leaders and others in the emergency tree. What details are needed at a moment's notice? Below is a list of those items that we have needed in times of a crisis:

- crisis management protocol
- participant medical information
- color photos of participants
- disclosed participant medical history
- passport numbers
- flight details
- emergency contact details at the university
- emergency contact details of the US Consulate or Embassy
- insurance contact details
- insurance forms
- domestic and international emergency phone numbers
- university forms

How can this be provided to faculty leaders without becoming cumbersome? Are faculty leaders and domestic personnel expected to carry this information around 24/7? It's likely that this information can be provided electronically on a flash drive, iPod, or online system that would make it accessible anywhere in the world where wireless internet is available. On some programs, computers and internet are not available, making printed material the only option. Providing the necessary details in as small a form as possible is of great help to faculty leaders. Also, consider what happens to this information once the program is over. Use the same scrutiny with electronic files as with paper.

7.3 Learning the Plan

With such a comprehensive CMP, orientation regarding crisis preparedness and planning is straightforward for faculty leaders and students. Still, training is necessary. Faculty leaders need to know what is expected of them, how to use the plan, and practice using the plan with sample scenarios. Faculty should also have the opportunity to ask questions. Students do not need to know the details of a university plan, but they do need to know that a plan exists and who they should contact first.

> A faculty leader was called after the study abroad office saw a Facebook post indicating that a student had an injury requiring first a wheelchair and then crutches. The university was not aware of what had happened to the student because there was no report from the faculty leader. The faculty leader refused to comply with university policy; he said the program was his and he was not required to inform the university. This was in violation of university policy. It also opened the university to possible legal action on behalf of the family.

By failing to follow university protocol in an emergency, faculty leaders take on personal liability that would otherwise be held by the university. The faculty leader, in effect, takes personal ownership of the program at that point. In such a case, the home university may prohibit the faculty leader from leading any more programs abroad and distance itself from the faculty leader if liability proceedings come to pass. At worst, the faculty may be directly sued by the student or the family.

> ### Case Study
>
> One morning at 6:00, a Study Abroad Director received a call from a program director abroad. The university partner on-site had received complaints from one of its own students that a staff member of the visiting delegation was sexually harassing her. Given the nature of the complaint, it was necessary to involve

the equal opportunity compliance office to ensure appropriate steps were followed. Since a long-standing university partner was involved, the President's Office was also notified and consulted. In addition, University Legal Counsel was consulted. The situation quickly became a delicate balance of ensuring our partner's satisfaction with the handling of the situation and respecting the rights of the home institution staff member.

- What are the sexual harassment policies in place at your university? Do they apply to study abroad programs?
- How would your university respond to program leaders? The staff member? The partner institution?

In all cases, it is vital that faculty leaders understand when to immediately contact the study abroad office and when it can wait. In this age of technology, it is likely a parent will know about an emergency before the study abroad office or even the faculty leader will know. On the other hand, this doesn't excuse faculty from acting outside the parameters of the CMP. It is embarrassing and risky for the study abroad office to receive a call from a parent, without knowledge of what has occurred.

When a 7.0 magnitude earthquake hit Haiti on January 12th, 2010, Lynn University had a group of 14 on the ground: two faculty and 12 students. It became evident almost immediately that several members of the group were missing. Lynn University wasted no time in setting up emergency notification on its university homepage, contacting the media, and dispatching staff to the Dominican Republic to help track the injured, hoping to find their missing students and faculty members. Unfortunately, for six members of their group, the crisis ended in tragedy. But the university acted quickly and spared no expense in doing what it could to assist in the effort to find its people. [10]

---

[10] Though the exact crisis website used by Lynn University is no longer active, they have created a page to inform the public of what took place and current response at www.lynn.edu/haiti.

7.4 Medical Information

It's a good idea for your university to request medical information from participants. This information can be processed through the health center, travel nurse, or study abroad office (if HIPAA and privacy issues are managed appropriately and faculty/staff fully understand the information). Medications have different names around the world, so be sure to obtain the locally marketed name for prescription drugs. Some international insurance companies have an online translation database for medical terms and brand name drugs. Working with an in-country contact can also help with finding this information before arrival.

A student who was insulin-dependent extended her program for several days. Since she had taken only enough insulin for the duration of the program, this left her without the medication she needed. The faculty leader worked with a local contact to find out what insulin was called locally and where it could be found.

The Health Insurance Portability and Accountability Act of 1996 (HIPAA) secures patient medical information. While it has been argued that requiring medical information violates HIPAA, the act specifically allows "the disclosure of personal health information needed for patient care."[11] Determine how this act is interpreted by the legal counsel of your institution. You cannot speak to a parent about the health of the student unless you have proper authorization by the student. You also cannot speak about the specific health situation to those in the crisis management tree at your institution. But students can voluntarily provide information to the faculty leader prior to departure. This helps prevent on-site emergencies since a faculty leader knows about the diabetic student or the student with a peanut allergy.

7.5 The Last Word

Crisis management is a scary thought for any new faculty leader and even seasoned study abroad officers. No one wants to learn that students are in trouble or danger. Having a serious discussion with your university to pre-determine support for crisis response and a course of action will define the various responsi-

---

[11] US Department of Health and Human Services, www.hhs.gov.

bilities of faculty leaders and university offices. Generally, the questions you should ask are:

- What does your campus deem a reportable emergency?
- Who do you call first in the event of an emergency?
- What funds are available to you and how quickly are they made available to you in an emergency?
- In what situations will insurance assist with emergency response? When will it not?
- What sort of documentation will your campus need? Will you issue a final written report following the crisis? Will you hold a debriefing session?
- What if the media call your office for a statement or interview regarding a particular crisis? How do you respond?

Know your university's CMP inside and out, and how to use it. Protect your students and yourself with knowledge, preparation, and communication for successful study abroad.

Resources

Professional Organizations
AIEA: Association of International Education Administrators. www.aiea.org

CIEE: Council on International Educational Exchange. www.ciee.org

The Forum on Education Abroad. www.forumea.org

NAFSA: Association of International Educators. www.nafsa.org

US Department of Education. "Family Educational Rights and Privacy Act (FERPA)." 5 May 2010. Web. 12 May 2010.

Study Abroad Office

Brockington, Joseph L., William W. Hoffa, and Patricia C. Martin, eds. *NAFSA's Guide to Education Abroad for Advisers and Administrators*. 3rd ed. Washington, DC: NAFSA, 2005. Print.

Burak, Patricia A., and William W. Hoffa, eds. *Crisis Management in a Cross-Cultural Setting*. Rev. ed. Washington, DC: NAFSA, 2001. Print.

Carlson, Jerry S., Barbara B. Burn, John Useem, and David Yachimowicz. *Study Abroad: The Experience of American Undergraduates*. New York: Greenwood Press, 1990. Print.

Facultyled.com. www.facultyled.com. Web.

Forum on Education Abroad, The. *Education Abroad Glossary*. Carlisle, PA: Forum, n.d. Print.

Hoffa, William W., and Stephen C. DePaul, eds. *A History of US Study Abroad: 1965 to Present*. a special publication of *Fron-*

tiers: The Interdisciplinary Journal of Study Abroad. n.p:
Frontiers, n.d. Print.

Spencer, Sarah E., and Kathy Tuma, eds. *The Guide to Successful
Short-Term Programs Abroad.* 2nd ed. Washington, DC: NAFSA,
2007. Print.

Williamson, Wendy. *Study Abroad 101.* 2nd ed. Charleston, IL:
Agapy, 2008. Print.

Faculty Orientation

Citron, James L. "Dr. Jim's Tips for Directors of US Students
Abroad." *International Educator.* May/June 2005: 64-66. Print.

----, and Rachel Kline. "From Experience to Experiential Education." *International Educator.* Fall 2001: 19-26. Print.

Hornig, James F. "The Toughest Job You'll Ever Love." *Academe.*
September-October 1995: 22-26. Print.

Krueger, Roberta L. "It's *Not* a Sabbatical." *Academe.* September-
October 1995: 31-34. Print.

MacNally, Susan, and Sarah E. Spencer. "Roles and Preparation
of Program Director." *The Guide to Successful Short-Term
Programs Abroad.* 2nd ed. Ed. Sarah E. Spencer and Kathy Tuma.
Washington, DC: NAFSA, 2007. 141-166. Print.

O'Neal, John C., "It's Like Wearing All the Hats." *Academe.* Sept.-
Oct. 1995: 28-31. Print.

Program Design and Development

Brick, Susan Holme, Lisa Chieffo, Tom Roberts, and Michael
Steinberg. "Planning, Budgeting, and Implementation." *NAFSA's
Guide to Education Abroad for Advisers and Administrators.*
Ed. Joseph L. Brockington, William W. Hoffa, and Patricia C.
Martin. 3rd ed. Washington, DC: NAFSA, 2005. 389-416. Print.

McKeachie, Wilbert J., and Marilla Svinicki. Teaching Tips; Strategies, research and Theory for College and University Teachers. Boston: Houghton Millflin, 2006. Print.

Rodman, Richard, and Martha Merrill. "Unlocking Study Abroad Potential: Design Models, Methods and Masters." *A History of US Study Abroad: 1965 to Present*. Ed. William W. Hoffa and Stephen C. DePaul. N.p.: Frontiers, n.d. 199-251. Print.

Spencer, Sarah, and Kathy Tuma, eds. *The Guide to Successful Short-Term Programs Abroad*. 2nd ed. Washington, DC: NAFSA, 2007. Print.

Stephenson, Skye, "The Program Director and the Program." *NAFSA's Guide to Education Abroad for Advisers and Administrators*. 3rd ed. Ed. Joseph L. Brockington, William W. Hoffa, Patricia C. Martin. Washington, DC: NAFSA, 2005. 539-552. Print.

Internationalization

Carley, Susan, Sutham Cheurprakobkit, and Daniel Paracka. "Faculty Attitudes Toward International Education: A Campus Experience." *Journal of Global Initiatives* 1.1. Spring 2006. 1-20. Print.

Lewin, Ross, ed. *The Handbook of Practice and Research in Study Abroad: Higher Education and the Quest for Global Citizenship*. New York: Routledge Taylor and Francis, 2009. Print.

Olson, Christa, Madeleine Green, Barbara Hill. A Handbook for Advancing Comprehensive Internationalization: What Institutions Can Do and What Students Should Learn. Washington, DC: ACE, 2006. Print.

Stearns, Peter N. *Educating Global Citizens in Colleges and Universities: Challenges and Opportunities*. New York: Routledge Taylor and Francis, 2009. Print.

Student Learning

Chieffo, Lisa, and Lesa Griffiths. "What's a Month Worth? Student Perceptions of What They Learned Abroad." *International Educator*. Fall 2003. 26-31. Print.

Cushner, Kenneth, and Ata U. Karim. "Study Abroad at the University Level." *Handbook of Intercultural Training*. 3rd ed. Ed. Dan Landis, Janet M. Bennett, and Milton J. Bennett. Thousand Oaks: Sage, 2004. 289-308. Print

Deardorff, Darla K., ed. *The SAGE Handbook of Intercultural Competence*. Los Angeles: SAGE, 2009. Print.

Dowell, Michelle-Marie, Kelly P. Mirsky. *Study Abroad: How to Get the Most Out of Your Experience*. Upper Saddle River: Prentice-Hall, 2003. Print.

Edwards, Natalie, and Christopher Hogarth. "Using Short-Term Study Abroad to Further Undergraduate Research." *Council on Undergraduate Research*. 29.2. Winter 2008. 14-17. Print.

Kepets, Dawn. *Back in the USA: Reflecting on Your Study Abroad Experience and Putting It to Work*. Sewickley, PA: NAFSA, 1995. Print.

Leki, Ray S. "Personal Skills: Beyond the Basics." *Travel Wise: How to Be Safe, Savvy and Secure Abroad*. Ray S. Leki. Boston: Intercultural Press, 2008. Print.

Lewis, Richard D. *When Cultures Collide: Leading Across Cultures*. 3rd ed. Boston: Nicholas Brealey International, 2006. Print.

Paige, R. Michael, Andrew D. Cohen, Barbara Kappler, Julie C. Chi, and James P. Lassegard. *Maximizing Study Abroad: A Students' Guide to Strategies for Language and Culture Learning and Use*. Minneapolis: University of Minnesota, 2002. Print.

---. *Maximizing Study Abroad: A Program Coordinators' Guide to Strategies for Language and Culture Learning and Use*. Minneapolis: University of Minnesota, 2002. Print.

Stewart, Edward C., and Milton J. Bennet. *American Cultural Patterns: A Cross-Cultural Perspective*. Rev. ed. Yarmouth: Intercultural Press, 1991. Print.

Sunnygard, John. "Program Leadership for Intercultural Development." *The Guide to Successful Short-Term Programs Abroad*. 2nd ed. Eds. Sarah E. Spencer and Kathy Tuma. N.p.: NAFSA, 2007 167-174. Print.

Ting-Toomey, Stella. *Communicating Across Cultures*. New York: Guilford Press, 1999. Print.

Glasser, William. *Choice Theory: A New Psychology of Personal Freedom*. New York: Harper Perennial, 1999. Print.

Health and Safety Resources
ASIRT: Association for Safe International Road Travel. www.asirt.org

CDC: Centers for Disease Control and Prevention. www.cdc.gov

Herrin, Carl, David Larsen, Barbara Lindeman, Patricia Martin, and Nancy Stubbs, eds. *Professional Practice Workshop: Safety and Responsibility in Education Abroad Participant Manual*. Washington, DC: NAFSA, 2006. Print.

IAMAT: The International Association for Medical Assistance to Travellers. www.iamat.org/index.cfm

Leki, Ray S. *Travel Wise: How to Be Safe, Savvy and Secure Abroad*. Boston: Intercultural Press, 2008. Print.

Kast, Richard C. "Promoting Health and Safety in Study Abroad." *International Educator*. 7.1. Fall 1997/Winter 1998. 25-32. Print.

Lindeman, Barbara, ed. *Best Practices in Addressing Mental Health Issues Affecting Education Abroad Participants*. N.p.: NAFSA, 2006. Web.

Lucas, John. "Over-Stressed, Overwhelmed, and Over Here: Resident Directors and the Challenges of Student Mental Health Abroad." *Frontiers: The Interdisciplinary Journal of Study Abroad*. 18. Fall 2009. 187-215. Print.

OSAC: Overseas Security Advisory Council. www.osac.gov

SAFETI Clearinghouse: Safety Abroad First Educational Travel Information. www.globaled.us/safeti

US Department of State. *Emergency Assistance to Americans Abroad*. Web. http://travel.state.gov

Liability

Rhodes, Gary, Robert Aalberts, William Hoye, and Joseph L. Brockington. "Legal Issues and Education Abroad." *NAFSA's Guide to Education Abroad for Advisers and Administrators*. 3rd ed. Ed. Joseph L. Brockington, William W. Hoffa, and Patricia C. Martin. Washington, DC: NAFSA, 2005. 511-533. Print.

Weeks, Kent. *Managing Liability and Overseas Programs*. Nashville: College Legal Information, Inc., 2001. Print.

Assessment

Bolen, Mell C., ed. *A Guide to Outcomes Assessment in Education Abroad*. N.p.: The Forum on Education Abroad, n.d. Print.

Braskamp, Larry A., David C. Braskamp, and Kelly C. Merrill. "Assessing Progress in Global Learning and Development of Students with Education Abroad Experiences." *Frontiers: The Interdisciplinary Journal of Study Abroad*. 18. Fall 2009. 187-215. Print.

Deardorff, Darla K., ed. *The SAGE Handbook of Intercultural Competence*. Los Angeles: SAGE, 2009. Print.

Doyle, Dennis. "Holistic Assessment and the Study Abroad Experience." *Frontiers: The Interdisciplinary Journal of Study Abroad.* 18. Fall 2009. 187-215. Print.

McLaughlin, Jacqueline S., and D. Kent Johnson. "Assessing the Field Course Experiential Learning Model: Transforming Collegiate Short-Term Study Abroad Experiences into Rich Learning Environments." *Frontiers: The Interdisciplinary Journal of Study Abroad.* 13. Nov 2006. 65-85 Print.

Sindt, Paige, and Ara Pachmayer. "Identifying the Outcomes of Short Term Study Abroad." *IIE Networker.* N.d. Web. 20 May 2010. www.iienetwork.org

Zukroff, Sacia, Stephen Ferst, Jennifer Hirsch, Carla Slawson, and Margaret Wiedenhoeft. "Program Assessment and Evaluation." *NAFSA's Guide to Education Abroad for Advisers and Administrators.* 3rd ed. Eds. Joseph L. Brockington, William W. Hoffa, and Patricia C. Martin. Washington, DC: NAFSA, 2005. 445-478. Print.

Index

Agapy Books and Resources
Study Abroad Division

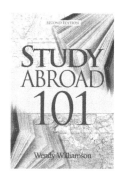

Study Abroad 101 has been completely revised and is nothing short of a masterpiece for the millennial student. This book presents everything US college students need to know about education abroad, from before they decide on a program to after they return, through 101 easy-to-navigate sections. It is highly recommended for students, advisors, faculty, orientations, and courses that prepare students to study abroad.

AbroadScout (www.abroadscout.com) – For students looking to study abroad, the website features excerpts from *Study Abroad 101* by Wendy Williamson and a top-notch programs directory with scholarships, student reviews, and more. Guests may submit non-promotional articles to be featured. The directory is search friendly, especially for faculty-led programs, and universities can create their own individualized program directories and tools.

Facultyled.com – For faculty who support travel-study abroad for internationalization and others interested in globalization, the future of higher education, and the 21st century university. Includes interesting articles for faculty leaders and international educators, an online faculty-led 101 guide, and a customized program provider directory. It also features excerpts from this book, and any updates.

CPSIA information can be obtained at www.ICGtesting.com
Printed in the USA
LVOW01s1204261113

362874LV00006B/362/P